Vashti M. McKenzie

JOURNEY
TO THE
WELL

Leader's Guide written by Alice J. Dise & Vanessa Ward
Edited by Katara Washington

Contributing Writers:
Alice Dise
Vanessa Ward

Edited by:
Katara Washington

Publisher
Urban Ministries, Inc.
P.O. Box 436987
Chicago, IL 60643-6987
1.800.860.8642

First Edition
First Printing
ISBN: 0-940955-78-4
Catalog No. 6-5420

TABLE OF CONTENTS

SESSION 1
A Woman With One Hope   15

SESSION 2
A Woman Open To God   25

SESSION 3
A Woman In Time   35

SESSION 4
A Woman Pregnant With The Possibilities Of God   45

SESSION 5
A Woman Breaking Down Barriers   55

SESSION 6
A Woman Overcomes Learned Ignorance   66

SESSION 7
A Woman Discovers A New Way Of Thinking   76

SESSION 8
A Woman Faces Her Past   88

SESSION 9
A Woman Without Excuses   100

SESSION 10
A Woman Takes An Opportunity   110

SESSION 11
A Woman Of Value And Worth   124

SESSION 12
A Woman With A Purpose   135

PREFACE

The Leader's Guide is designed for use with the devotional book *Journey To The Well.*

Throughout the Scriptures, God has done some wonderful and miraculous works for people who have gathered at the well. Daily, shepherds gathered their flocks and drew water from the well. Daily, travelers sojourning from one location to another in the hot and dry climate, drew water from the well. Daily, the women gathered, in keeping with their traditional role, at the well, to draw the water that would help them carry out all of the activities that would physically sustain them and their families for the day.

So common a place was the well, yet in many instances as God destined, so transformative a place became the well. The Scriptures record that God met those shepherds, sojourners and women at the well; and when God met them, God changed them and their circumstances, and they were no longer the same. One by one, God touched their lives and each experienced life-transformative moments—break-throughs, that took their ordinary circumstances and made them extraordinary.

Journey to the Well focuses, in particular, on one of those transformative—breakthrough—well moments: the experience of the Samaritan woman at the well, that is found in the Gospel of John 4:1-30, 39. What Jesus offered to her—water which would make her thirst no more—is made available to each of us as we journey to the well.

Many of us are in need of God's transformative power in our lives. We have been living life only concerned with our physical sustenance: food, water, shelter, success, etc. Yet we have felt the emptiness of such living and desire to be filled spiritually. How do we receive the spiritual fulfillment God promises? Where can we find that well in which Jesus promises to give water that makes us thirst no more? How do we receive that living water and keep it in our lives?

This study is designed to help individuals answer these questions by presenting a basic, step-by-step approach to disciplined spiritual journeying. The "journey to the well" is an invitation to discipline the mind and the spirit. By following the Disciplines of the Well, individuals are taken deeper in their faith walk and guided toward finding their personal experience of spiritual fulfillment.

The purpose of this Leader's Guide is to direct and assist leaders who wish to use Journey to the Well for group Bible study. Each Bible study participant should have a copy of the book, Journey to the Well and the Student Workbook. Both the Leader's Guide and Student Workbook are organized in 12 Bible study sessions that correspond to the 12 chapters of the devotional book. The Leader's Guide and Student Workbook provide Disciplines of the Well for each session that will guide participants through their spiritual journey.

There are five segments to the Disciplines of the Well through which the leaders guide students to follow for each session:

- **Well Lessons** – the focus on questions, activities and points for discussion that emerge from the Scripture passage. Students are asked questions about what actually happened to the Samaritan woman in the passage. Students are given two to four well lessons which spring up from the Samaritan woman's experience and they are encouraged to follow these lessons in their own personal spiritual journey.

- **Well Words** – the focus on related Scriptures that allow participants to examine the Word of God and explore the biblical truths for themselves. These biblical truths frame the journey and serve as landmarks providing direction. Students are encouraged to memorize at least one of these well words for each session.

- **Well Sabbaticals** – the focus of the journey that centers the study on the meditation of Scriptures, a specific biblical theme, and prayer. It is a regular period of rest and reflection in which you deliberately slow down the pace of living and disconnect from everything, except the presence of God.

- **Well Language** – words of positive affirmation are presented that students can use to encourage them on their journey. Students are encouraged to select at least one of these positive affirmations, write it on a 3x5 or 5x7 card with a felt-tip pen in the color preferred, and post it where the student frequents. This affirmation can also be shared with others.

•**Well Works** – students are encouraged to evaluate their personal walk with God and challenged to apply the Word of God in their lives by selecting at least one activity that demonstrates progress in their personal journey to the well. Well Works are simple, practical exercises to help the student go deeper through application and demonstration of lessons learned on the journey.

This Leader's Guide will direct you in the following format, which incorporates the Five Disciplines for each session:

- **Lesson Aims** – outline goals that each participant should meet by the end of each session.

PART ONE

- **Opening Prayer** – invites reflections on Well Sabbaticals experienced and includes specific prayers for participants.
- **Scripture Search** – questions, activities, and points for discussion on the selected Scripture passage from John 4.
- **Chapter Highlights** – selected definitions and an outline of chapter topics to facilitate review and discussion in a group setting.

PART TWO

- This is the **Bible Study Application** Section that includes time for group discussion of each Well Lesson and contains multiple part questions which allow participants to examine several Scriptures that reinforce the teachings of each of the Well Lessons presented.
- **Life Application** Section that consists of Personal Application Questions and Church Ministry Application Questions:
  - Personal Application Questions – Well Words, Well Language and Well Works are presented to encourage participants to evaluate their personal walk with God and challenge them to apply the Word of God in their own lives.
  - Church Ministry Application Questions – are presented to encourage participants to incorporate the teachings of each lesson in their local church and ministries.
- **Closing Prayer**

In summary, the Leader's Guide contains recommended structure, background information, related activities, and answers to the Bible Study Application questions for each session of the Bible Study. Bible Background sections are included in selected chapters and provide pertinent information that enhances the overall Bible Study experience. Due to the nature of the Life Application discussion, answers for the Personal Application and the Church Ministry Application questions are not provided.

Uses. Although this Leader's Guide is designed to facilitate a group study, it can be used in a variety of ways. This book can be used for both personal and family devotions conducted in private, home-study groups or within the local church setting. The Leader's Guide can be used to train teachers, officers and clergy on the disciplines of spiritual journeying. Training can take place as a selected curriculum for use:

- during Sunday School as an elective course
- during the church's weekly Training Hour
- as a weekday Bible Study on spiritual growth
- as an Adult Vacation Bible School class
- as an excellent source for a women's Bible Study course
- as an exciting study for a joint men's and women's class that would allow for a rich dialogue of shared feelings and challenges.

Group Study – 90 Minute Sessions. A 90-minute group session is divided into two parts. In Part One, participants discuss the Scripture Search and Chapter Highlights. During Part Two, the session leader divides the group into smaller groups to answer and discuss the Bible Study Application questions, which focus on the Well Lessons for each session. The small group discussions provide each participant with an opportunity to contribute to the group's understanding and application of the material. In the final discussion, the participants reconvene with the larger group to report their findings and review the Life Application questions

Group Study – 60 Minute Sessions. The 60-Minute group sessions are divided into the same two parts as the 90-minute session, but eliminate Chapter Highlights and Life Application Sections. Participants discuss the Scripture, Well Lessons, and the related background information during the group meeting. If time permits, selected Life Application questions can be used as a stimulus for discussion, or used as a "homework" assignment or for private devotional study.

Church-Wide Retreats and Leadership Training.

When all or part of a weekend is available, a study in *Journey to the Well* can be conducted in a number of ways. For example, twelve people could be assigned to lead a workshop on a different chapter. Participants would read the entire book prior to the retreat or scheduled training. Then, they would be encouraged to select a chapter to study in depth and attend the workshop devoted to that chapter.

In the opening session, the overall leader (pastor, minister, special speaker, or lay leader) would give a presentation on the theme: "The Importance of The Journey to the Well: Developing a Disciplined Spiritual Life," to set the tone and focus of the study. This presentation should focus on defining Well Disciplines and challenging participants to examine and apply these disciplines to their daily lives. Finally, emphasis should focus on the benefits that such disciplines will bring to their local church setting.

After the opening session, participants would attend the workshops that focus on a particular chapter. These sessions should include general discussion, personal application, and produce specific suggestions and/or strategies for church ministry.

The final session would be devoted to small group discussion and reports. These reports should be given by representatives from each workshop. This final discussion would also involve sharing the answers to the Church Ministry Application section of each chapter. These suggestions may be used to plan activities for the upcoming church calendar year.

Family Devotions.

Before the study of a particular chapter, each member would read the chapter privately and do the Bible Study Application questions. In devotions, the family would first discuss the chapter. Then each member could present his or her answers, opinions, and insights. The devotion should end with personal application and prayer.

Preparing Participants for the Discussion.

To prepare for each Well Session, participants should read the assigned chapter of the student devotional book, *Journey to the Well*. Encourage participants to take time to do all of the Disciplines of the Well before each session, meditate, pray, and carefully study the assigned material. Ask them to come prepared to share reflections, Scriptures, or experiences related to the information presented in each chapter. Note: Because of the personal reflections which many of the participants may experience as they deepen their spiritual walk, the leader must be prayerful for discernment and guidance in providing support and compassion for the sharing of sensitive issues. Leaders must provide a supportive and trusting atmosphere for participants to share freely.

Leading the Discussion.

Several techniques can be used to lead group discussions. Effective leadership always requires good preparation. Begin by reading *Journey to the Well* from beginning to end. Take notes, underline interesting or important passages, jot down ideas which come to you. ***FOLLOW THE DISCIPLINES OF THE WELL** for each session, so that you will be able to genuinely share in the transformative experience that this journey invites its participants to share.*

Before each Bible Study session:
1. Pray for wisdom.
2. Know the goal.
3. Depend on the Holy Spirit.
4. Reflect on the Disciplines of the Well that you have followed in preparation for teaching this class. Review the personal surprises you found, the challenges you met, the celebrations you experienced.
5. Gather any supplies or additional information you may need.

During each session:
1. Begin with prayer.
2. Maintain a relaxed, informal atmosphere.
3. Keep track of the time.
4. Keep the discussion moving by asking probing questions, restating the topic, and pointing out the differences between the world's view and God's view.
5. Focus on the Well Lessons and Well Words.
6. Encourage participants to evaluate their lifestyles, goals, and objectives and to apply the biblical truths to their own lives so that they can apply their Well Works in the world today.

THE DISCIPLINES DEFINED

It's important that the Leader understands completely the Disciplines of the Well, so that the students are encouraged to follow them to experience the maximum effectiveness intended during their journey.

In the devotional book *Journey to the Well*, the term "discipline" is defined as *a simple ordering and organizing of behavior according to a specific structure with a determined outcome in mind.*

As the Leader, it is important for you to share with students that the road to deepened spiritual fulfillment is accomplished through a disciplined spiritual life. That disciplined spiritual life must be marked by determined outcomes—a closer walk with Jesus, a desire to spend more time in the word of God, a prioritizing of time spent with the Word of God, an applied faith in daily living, a deepened understanding of self worth, role and responsibility to the kingdom mission.

Those determined outcomes will force a serious student to set goals, make plans, aspire to reach new heights, and FOCUS! It is impossible to reach deepened spiritual fulfillment and growth without discipline.

> *Determined outcomes force me to set goals, make plans, aspire to reach new heights and focus!* — *Vashti Mckenzie*

The five Disciplines of the Well outlined in this Bible study assist participants in reaching determined outcomes in personal spiritual fulfillment and growth. Let's explore each of the disciplines and the determined outcomes for each.

I. WELL LESSONS: The Foundation of Your Journey

The Leader must read and study the scriptural text for each lesson. The text will be the focus for the Bible Study for each session. Participants will be asked to describe the events that took place in the life of the Samaritan woman.

It will be important for the Leader to read all background Scriptures that bring understanding of the context in which the woman lived and the Bible truths that emerged from those texts.

Reflect on the two to four well lessons given for each session. These are important lessons that can support the participant's journey and provide the biblical foundation necessary. In this discipline, participants are asked to reflect on what ways the story parallels their story; what did she do? What should I do when given similar circumstances? What biblical truth is God trying to tell me through the reading and reflection on this word?

DETERMINED OUTCOMES:
1. Identify The Biblical Truths Found In The Scriptures
Read the Scripture outlined for each session. Reflect on what the Samaritan woman experienced. Read supporting Scriptures that emphasize the teachings of each lesson. Reflect on the messages revealed through those Scriptures.

2. Reflect On What They Mean To My Life Personally
Reflect on ways in which the Samaritan woman's experience parallels your experience(s) in life? In what ways did you act as she acted? In what ways should you have acted? What lessons do the supporting Scriptures encourage you to receive?

In reviewing the things that happened to her, we can first attempt to put ourselves into her shoes.
- In what ways does her story parallel our story?
- How does she feel?
- How do I feel?
- What did she do?
- What would I have done differently? Why?
- What would I have done similarly? Why?

II. WELL WORDS: The Framing Of Your Journey

The Well Words are biblical references that have been selected to help guide the spiritual journey of the participant.

The Word of God will be "A lamp unto my feet and a light unto my path."
                                                          –Psalms 119:105

Leader must guide the participants in recognizing the importance of reading the Word of God daily and committing that word to memory so that it can be "hidden in their hearts."
There are many obstacles that can deter us on our journey in life, but the Word

of God will keep us grounded and enable us to remain on the path that God has intended us to follow.

For each session, participants are given Well Words, Scriptures from which they may select at least one to memorize.

DETERMINED OUTCOME:
1. The Importance Of The Word Of God Will Be Acknowledged
The Word of God will be acknowledged as guidance and light.

Participants will seek to study it daily and memorize it so that it will be placed deep in their heart and soul and made applicable to their lives when they most need it!

111. THE WELL SABBATICAL: The Focus of Your Journey

At the outset, it is important to note that the term sabbatical (*shabaq* or *shabat* Hebrew verb) is a biblical word and concept that occurs throughout the Bible. Its principal meaning is defined as *leave, let alone; to cease, to abstain, to terminate, to be an end.* Its secondary usage means *to be inactive; to rest.* The secondary usage, of which many of us are familiar, has been a necessary practice that has encouraged rest from hectic and demanding schedules and lifestyles.

In reading the Bible, we find several ways in which the word Sabbatical is used. First, it is used primarily to dictate a legal mandate for all to abstain from physical labor—to rest and observe the seventh day of the week as a day of sabbath to the Lord. On this day, there was to be no work done by father, son, daughter, manservant, maidservant, land nor animal. It was a day that was to be observed with reverence. Read Exodus 16:22-30; Exodus 20:2-17, Exodus 23:10-19; Exodus 34:21; Deuteronomy 5:6-18; Leviticus 26:34-35; and 1 Corinthians 16:2 for examples of sabbaticals defined as abstaining from all physical labor, both agricultural and commercial.

Later, sabbatical is used to describe a day of positive worship of God, which consisted of not only the complete abstention from all labor but also the gathering of the saints in the temple or synagogue for prayer, sacrifice and ritual observances. Read Leviticus 19:3, 30 for the meaning of sabbath as a cultic or worship institution.

Participants in this study are encouraged to take deliberate times of rest—to abstain from all labor and remove distractions so that they might focus on God and experience worship with God.

DETERMINED OUTCOMES:

1. Identified Space And Time With The Lord

Students will begin by identifying a private and personal space and specific time where no one else is permitted to enter during the sabbatical.

2. Focused Thoughts And Reflections

Students will be led to focus thoughts on specific biblical texts and biblical themes. Students should be encouraged to not take this time as a slumbering event - an opportunity to watch TV, talk on the phone, take kids to school, sit in front of the computer, listen to the radio or a CD.

> It is intentional time to listen to the silence, smell the atmosphere, taste the moments as they pass by, and get in touch with your innermost thoughts.
> —Vashti McKenzie

Each session will identify steps or stepping stones that participants are encouraged to take for each sabbatical. Leaders should encourage students to observe each stepping stone, keep a journal, and share reflections during the group session.

IV. WELL LANGUAGE: The Firming Of Your Journey

The Well Language consists of positive phrases and thoughts that are reflective of the Well Lessons and Well Words presented in each session. These positive phrases provide affirmations on which the participant can focus to gain support for the journey.

DETERMINED OUTCOMES:

1. Select Positive Affirmations To Surround You

Participants are given a list of positive phrases for each session. At least one phrase is selected, written on a 3 x 5 or 5 x 7 card and placed in a location where the participants frequent. For example, cards could be placed on the refrigerator door, the bathroom mirror, or the desk at work. The placement of the cards ensures that they will frequently be reminded of the positive and affirming messages that each card brings.

2. Share Positive Affirmations With Others

The Leader should encourage participants to share their affirmations with others. Shared positive thinking enhances the participants' witness and spiritual walk.

V. WELL WORKS: The Footwork Of Your Journey

The Leader should encourage participants to demonstrate the lessons learned in the *Journey to the Well*, by selecting at least one of the suggested practical exercises given for each session. These exercises invite participants to apply the lessons learned in their everyday contemporary experiences.

DEMONSTRATED OUTCOME:
Application Of Lessons Learned

For each session, a list of suggested practical exercises, Well Works, are provided. Participants must choose one or more Well Work(s) to apply daily in their lives. Practice of these activities allows for a demonstration of lessons learned.

Don't just talk the talk...
WALK IT!!!!!

A WOMAN WITH ONE HOPE

For sessions of 90 minutes or more, use the lesson format for PART ONE and PART TWO.

PART ONE

Opening Prayer - 5 minutes

Scripture - 10 minutes

Chapter Highlights* - 20 minutes

PART TWO

Well Lessons

Small Group - 20 minutes

Large Group - 15 minutes

Life Application* - 15 minutes

Closing Prayer - 5 minutes

*Chapter Highlights and Life Application Sections are eliminated in 60-minute Sessions

For sessions of less than 90 minutes, the Life Application questions may be assigned as homework.

Once upon a well there was a woman, a Samaritan woman singularly stepping through the swirls of dust. She is on a mission to get water from Jacob's well. Heat penetrates the ordinary weave of her robe. Her face is covered by tradition. Her eyes are lowered by culture. Her hands clutch an empty pot carrying one hope. That hope being that one day, things would change.
—Vashti McKenzie

Lesson Aim

At the end of this Bible study session, the participants should be able to: a) examine Jesus' response to the Samaritan woman's one-hope situation; b) realize that Jesus will intentionally meet each one of us in our one-hope situations; c) consider their personal response to one-hope situations; d) realize that it is often in the midst of one-hope situations that we are able to see the handiwork of God; and e) make a commitment to expect

Jesus to change our one-hope situations from the ordinary to the extraordinary.

"Now faith is being sure of what we hope for and certain of what we do not see" (Hebrews 11:1, NIV).

PART ONE

OPENING PRAYER – 5 minutes

Open the session with a prayer of thanksgiving for the Disciplines of the Well and the varied Well Sabbaticals that the participants will experience in this study. Pray that God will bless each participant to:

- Understand the importance of one-hope situations to Christian living.
- Consider the times that Jesus met them in a one-hope situation and how they benefited from that encounter.
- Make a commitment to expect Jesus to meet them and to change their one-hope situations.

SCRIPTURE SEARCH – 10 minutes

Ask for a volunteer to read John 4:1-7a and Romans 8:24-25 aloud to the group, and others to answer the following questions:

1. Under what circumstances did Jesus go through Samaria?
While in Judea, Jesus became aware that the Pharisees were discussing the number of disciples He was winning and baptizing and Jesus decided to leave Judea and go to Galilee to avoid any potential disputes (vv. 1-3).

Also, verse 4 seems to indicate that Jesus was compelled or divinely led to go through Samaria, as it records that Jesus went through Samaria because *He needed to go* (v. 4).

2. Why did Jesus decide to stop at Jacob's well?
Jesus had been traveling a distance and became tired, so He sat down. The place where He sat was Jacob's well (v. 5).

3. At what time did the Samaritan woman come to draw water at Jacob's well?
It was about the sixth hour (v. 6). The sixth hour would have been around 12 noon since the Jewish day began at 6 a.m. and ended at 6 p.m.

4. Why does hope need to be unseen?
If we saw it, we wouldn't have to hope for it. We'd already have evidence or proof (Romans 8:24).

5. How are we instructed to wait for what we do not see?
Patiently (v. 25)

CHAPTER HIGHLIGHTS –
20 minutes (recommended for 90-minute sessions only)
Using the content of Chapter 1 of the Devotional book as background, give a general overview of the chapter. Be sure to include the following topics:
1. Having one last hope (living with the desire that one day, things will change) keeps us going.
2. One-hope situations reveal the handiwork of God
3. We experience transformation through one-hope situations.

Bible Background: One-Hope Situations!
Have the class read 1 Kings 17:1-16 and engage the class in a brief discussion on the following:
Summarize Elijah's reason for fleeing to the brook called Cherith. Discuss God's miraculous provision for his one hope situation.
Then discuss how God led Elijah to another one-hope situation involving the widow at Zarephath.
Discuss how Elijah's attitude or level of faith may have changed when he experienced the widow of Zarephath's one-hope situation. Would his previous one-hope situation have helped him trust God more?
How does Ephesians 3:20 relate to Elijah and the widow's one-hope situations?

PART TWO

BIBLE STUDY APPLICATION
Introduction
The Bible Study Application section contains three Well Lessons that provide an opportunity to examine what the Bible says about one-hope situations and how we can apply these principles to our lives today. The discussion of the Well Lessons should confirm that the students understand the basic principles of living through

one-hope situations. Allow as much time as necessary to encourage free participation and exchange of ideas and insights.

Procedure

Select Small Group Leaders. Ask for volunteers or select three small group leaders and assign each one a number from 1-3. Ask the small group leaders to write their number on large sheets of white paper so that they can be seen from a distance.. (This can also be done beforehand to save time.)

Divide into Small Groups. Inform the participants that they will be separated into small groups. Each group will reflect on a different Well Lesson and then present their reflections to the larger group at the end of the study period. The Well Lessons should be assigned as follows:

Group 1: Hold fast to that last hope. (Well Lesson #1)

Group 2: When down to the last hope, look for Jesus to meet you there and to change your situation and to change you. (Well Lesson #2)

Group 3: Celebrate one hope at a time as you journey to your own well. (Well Lesson #3)

Allow Participants to Count Off by Threes. Then ask them to follow the small group leader who is holding their assigned number. Identify the location of each group. (These locations can also be pre-printed on a sheet of paper, photocopied, and distributed to save time.) Participants should then gather into smaller groups in the designated meeting areas.

Note: If the Bible Study is large, divide into more groups and reassign alternately the same three Well Lessons to each of the additional groups. In this case, possibly more than one group will be reflecting on each of the Well Lessons. If the Bible Study is small, divide into two groups and permit each group to discuss as many of the reflections as each group desires.

Small Group Study

Small Group Leaders

Each group will have one Well Lesson to explore. For each Well Lesson, there are questions and/or related Scripture references to stimulate discussion.

Sharing Insights

After 15 minutes, designate someone to summarize the small group discussion within the large group presentation that follows. The designated person should have three to five minutes to present.

Large Group Presentations

Reconvene the Group. Call the small groups together.

Explain the Procedure. A representative from each of the small groups will share that group's reflections on the assigned Well Lesson. The large group will present an opportunity to comment on reflections after all presentations have been made. Remind participants of the large group to be attentive and jot down notes or significant points on which comments may be made at the designated time.

Remind Small Group Representatives of the Time. Each group representative should summarize the group's reflection in less than five minutes. Allow up to five minutes to discuss each group's presentation.

Note: If there are more than three groups, allow each group three minutes to summarize reflections and encourage small group presenters to keep their reflections within the three minutes.

LIFE APPLICATION DISCUSSION*

If time permits, the larger group can then discuss reflections on the Well Words, Well Language and Well Works sections of their workbook.

Introduction

The Life Application section consists of reflections on the Well Words, Well Language, and Well Works described in the Student Book. Participants are asked to share which words (Scriptures) personally framed their journey, which language or affirmations they considered to be personally helpful and what steps they would personally take to demonstrate the lessons learned. Finally, students should be encouraged to engage themselves in the activities of the Well Works. Discussion should also address the implications for the church as a whole.

Sharing Insights

This discussion should be open-ended and voluntary. The sharing of personal insights or recommendations for church ministry should be encouraged but not required. The group may have much to share. Be mindful of the time and dedicate only 15 minutes to this exercise.

*Answers are not provided for this section of the study because of the personal or specific nature of the reflections.

Preparation For Next Meeting

Assignment. Participants are asked to read Chapter 2, "A Woman Open to God." Review the Well Lessons in preparation for the next session. Encourage them to come prepared to share their insights on the content of the next chapter.

The Leader may also want to assign small groups or specific Well Lessons to facilitate next week's meeting time.

CLOSING PRAYER

Form a prayer circle and invite all to pray individually for the courage to surrender their last-hope situation to Jesus. Leader closes this prayer time with a prayer of thanksgiving for the deliverance of God's people.

ANSWERS TO BIBLE STUDY APPLICATION

WELL LESSON #1
Hold on to that last hope.

1. Read Romans 8:24b, 25, NIV - "But hope that is seen is no hope at all. Who hopes for what he already has? But if we hope for what we do not yet have, we wait for it patiently."

The key words regarding hope in this lesson are "wait" and "patiently." Write your interpretation of why these two elements are vital to a last-hope situation. **Waiting patiently implies that one is certain that the outcome will be "good." "And we know that in all things God works for the good of those who love him ..." (Romans 8:28a, NIV).**

2. Read Hebrews 11:1, NIV - "Now faith is being sure of what we hope for and certain of what we do not see."

The key word in this passage is "faith." What part might it play in helping one to hold fast to his/her last hope? Find an example of how a Bible character used faith to hold fast to his/her last hope. **Faith requires a proper basis for existence. It requires knowing in whom your faith is based. Job said, "I will wait for my renewal to come" (Job 14:14), implying his certainty of the pending change.**

WELL LESSON #2

Look for Jesus to meet you at the well to change your situation and to change you.

Many of us live with one hope. We all have at least one hope, one fragile idea, one fragment of potential, one piece of possibility we carry around with us like a Samaritan woman carries empty water pots to a well.—Vashti McKenzie

When we find ourselves down to our last hope and are earnestly seeking a day when things will change, we must look for the presence of Jesus. Jesus will meet us in our last-hope situations. The following Scripture references point to instances where Jesus showed up and turned last hope situations into promising moments of purpose and fulfillment.

1. Read the following Scripture references and write how Jesus met people at their last-hope situations and changed them.

Luke 8:43-48
Jesus was the last hope for the woman with the issue of blood. He healed her.

Mark 5:1-20
Jesus was the last hope for the demon-possessed man. He commanded the demons to come out of him.

Matthew 8:23-27
Jesus was the last hope for the disciples in the boat. He calmed the storm.

Mark 5:35-43
Jesus was the last hope for Jairus, whose daughter was dead. Jesus raised her.

Luke 23:40-43
Jesus was the last hope for the thief on the cross. Jesus promised that he'd be with Him in paradise.

WELL LESSON #3
Celebrate one hope at a time as you journey to your own well.

Celebrating while we journey to the well, seeking help for our last hope situations can be difficult. How do the following Scriptures encourage us to celebrate while we hope and wait patiently?

Romans 8:28
Even the last hope situations we're in are working together for our good.

James 2:2-4
These situations are testing our faith and the test will help develop perseverance, which will make us mature and complete.

1 Thessalonians 5:16-18
It is God's will for us to celebrate and to give thanks for all situations and circumstances.

LIFE APPLICATION
Personal Application
Reflect on ways that you have been faced with last-hope situations. How did you feel? Where did you go? To whom or to what did you turn?

How can remembering these last-hope situations help you when you face another last-hope situation?

WELL WORDS
We must remember to turn to Jesus. He desires to meet us in our last hope situations, and often Jesus speaks to us through the Word of God. The following Well Words are offered as encouragement when you feel that you are in the midst of a last-hope situation. Select one Well Word per day or per week. Memorize this Well Word. It is your personal spiritual landmark to help you in your journey.

"For I know the plans I have for you," declares the Lord, "plans to prosper you and not to harm you, plans to give you hope and a future" (Jeremiah 29:11, NIV).

"Now faith is being sure of what we hope for and certain of what we do not see" (Hebrews 11:1, NIV).

"... But those who hope in the Lord will renew their strength" (Isaiah 40:31, NIV).

"...Put your hope in God, for I will yet praise Him, my Savior..." (Psalm 42:5, NIV).

"We have this hope as an anchor for the soul, firm and secure..." (Hebrews 6:19, NIV).

"Be joyful in hope, patient in affliction, faithful in prayer" (Romans 12:12, NIV).

WELL SABBATICAL

It is intentional time to listen to the silence, smell the atmosphere, taste the moments as they pass by, and get in touch with your innermost thoughts. — *Vashti McKenzie*

Write in your travel log or journal about a time when you had only "one hope." Write about a time when you were down to your "last something." Spend five minutes meditating on the hymn, "My Hope is Built On Nothing Less."

My Hope is Built On Nothing Less

"My hope is built on nothing less than Jesus' blood and righteousness;

I dare not trust the sweetest frame, but wholly lean on Jesus' name.

His oath, His covenant, His blood support me in the overwhelming flood;

When all around my soul gives way, He then is all my hope and stay.

On Christ the solid rock I stand. All other ground is sinking sand.

All other ground is sinking sand."

("My Hope is Built" AME Hymnal, p. 364, Words: Edward Mote; Music: William B. Broadbury)

Be prepared to share your reflections during this Sabbatical with your class.

WELL LANGUAGE

Let the following affirmations of encouragement also guide you in your journey. Write your favorite on a 3x5 or 5x7 file card in a felt-tip pen in a color you prefer.

1. One day, things will change
2. Hope is the key that unlocks the door
3. If I have hope, I have help.
4. If you have hope, you have help.
5. With God, nothing is impossible.
6. I am confident in the name of Jesus Christ.
7. I am capable of doing all things through Christ, who strengthens me.
8. Because of Christ, I am confident that I can respond to knowledge,
9. information, events and challenges in my life.
10. Carry on, you can make it!

WELL WORKS

The following Well Works are provided to help you take steps to demonstrate your new commitment to live out the lessons learned in this session. Choose one or more Well Works to do during a day:

1. Make a list of your own last things.
2. Read 1 Kings 17.
3. Start your collage. Select your surface: a large board, poster board, cork board, canvas, bulletin board, wall or large drawing pad. Be creative. Collect images and objects that remind you of your one hope and mount them on your collage surface.
4. Write in your journal about when you were down to your last things. Also write about what is the one thing you are hoping for now.

Church Ministry Application

- Does your church encourage its members to be community-oriented and reach out to those persons in one-hope situations? If not, why?
- List programs within your church that meet those needs?
- How can sharing our personal testimonies about one-hope situations help others? What are some of the barriers of sharing our testimonies?

A WOMAN OPEN TO GOD

For sessions of 90 minutes or more, use the lesson format for PART ONE and PART TWO.

PART ONE

Opening Prayer - 5 minutes

Scripture - 10 minutes

Chapter Highlights* - 20 minutes

PART TWO

Well Lessons

Small Group - 20 minutes

Large Group - 15 minutes

Life Application* - 15 minutes

Closing Prayer - 5 minutes

*Chapter Highlights and Life Application Sections are eliminated in 60-minute Sessions

For sessions of less than 90 minutes, the Life Application questions may be assigned as homework.

Any encounter can be an encounter with the Divine.
—*Vashti McKenzie*

Lesson Aim

This Bible study session will help participants to understand that: a) God meets us where we are — when we are open to healing. b) realize that sharing personal experiences, though painful, with others like yourself, will break barriers of disconnection. The healing community can be the point of embarkation; c) appreciate times of God's intervention in our lives, knowing there are no accidents with God.

"Now he had to go through Samaria" (John 4:4, NIV).

PART ONE

OPENING PRAYER – 5 minutes

Open the session by asking a volunteer for a prayer of thanksgiving for God's presence in our past well experiences. You or another volunteer may conclude the prayer. Pray that God will help each participant to:

- Realize that whatever happens to them is of importance to God.
- Begin to dismantle the barriers to healing by connecting with members of the faith community.
- Believe in the possibility of God's intervention even in our last-hope situations.

SCRIPTURE SEARCH – 10 Minutes

Ask someone to read the Samaritan woman's story, focusing on John 4:4-9, 19, 25, 28-29, and present the following questions to the class. Allow for discussion.

1. In what way does the story of the Samaritan woman in John 4 relate to the words of Jesus recorded in Luke 19:10?—"For the Son of Man came to seek and to save what was lost."
Jesus' trip to Samaria was an example of seeking lost persons; i.e., the woman herself, and other Samaritans who would be touched by the message of the Messiah that she would carry back to her village.

2. What are the indications in the story that the Samaritan woman wanted to be cut off from everyone?
She chose the worst time of day to go to the well. Other persons were unlikely to be at the well during the hottest part of the day.

3. What indications exist to show that she was open to God?
There was a progression of respect as she became aware of who Jesus really was. She began by referring to Him as a Jew, then Sir, then Prophet, and finally she mentions expectations of the Messiah. Also, when she was certain that Jesus could help her, she did not resist His offer for help, and she told others about Him.

CHAPTER HIGHLIGHTS –
20 Minutes (recommended for 90-minute sessions only)
Discuss the following topics:
1. God is able to meet us in both the ordinary and the extraordinary.
2. Remain open to God and pay attention to what He is saying.
3. Reconnect with the Samaritans and the other brothers and sisters in our lives.

Bible Background: There Are No Chance Meetings With God

It is important to note that Jesus intentionally went through Samaria to meet the Samaritan woman in her one-hope situation.

Ask the class, "How do we know that Jesus' going through Samaria was intentional and not coincidental? Participants should mention the following in their responses:

Jesus decided to go through Samaria even though Jews did not customarily associate with Samaritans (John 4:9).

There was another route to Galilee. Even though it was a longer route, most Jews would have taken the longer route to avoid encountering any Samaritans.

The animosity was so great among them that they avoided, hated and despised each other. It was remarkable that Jesus would decide to go through the city of the despised Samaritans, rather than avoid a potentially dangerous encounter by deciding to take another route.

Ask someone to read 2 Kings 17:24-34 aloud to the group. This passage describes why the Jews despised the Samaritans. Discuss the following:

The actions of the king of Assyria (2 Kings 17:24)

The replacement of some Israelites and the intermarriage of other Israelites with foreigners and their gods (2 Kings 17:27-29)

Point out that Jesus spoke to the Samaritan woman, even though as a Jew, Jesus was culturally prohibited from speaking to her.

She was a woman. Culturally, how were women regarded?

She was a Samaritan. Culturally, how were Jews to regard Samaritans? (John 4:7-9).

Reflect on the hour in which the Samaritan woman came. It was high noon (the 6th hour of the day) and usually the women drew water early in the morning and late in the evening to avoid the extreme heat of the day.

This woman chose to go to the well when no other women were present—perhaps to avoid their comments about her lifestyle.

By choosing this hour, she would most likely avoid having to see anyone

Point out that Jesus disregarded the cultural restrictions that prevented Jews and Samaritans from associating with each other by intentionally deciding to pass through Samaria; and disregarding the cultural restrictions that prevented Jewish men from talking to women. Jesus demonstrated how He will go to great measures to meet us in our time of need, even when we try to be invisible.

PART TWO

BIBLE STUDY APPLICATION

Introduction

The Bible Study Application section contains two Well Lessons that will help determine best ways and reasons to be open to God. The discussion of the Well Lessons should be an encouragement for students to be open to God. Allow free discussion, including personal experiences.

Procedure

Select Small Group Leaders. Ask for volunteers or select two small group leaders and assign each leader a number from 1-2. (You may separate each question under the 2 well lessons to make 4 groups) Ask the small group leaders to write their number on large sheets of white paper so that they can be seen from a distance. (This can also be done beforehand to save time.)

Divide into Small Groups. Inform the participants that they will be separated into small groups. Each group will reflect on a different Well Lesson and then present their reflections to the larger group at the end of the study period. The Well Lessons should be assigned as follows:

Group 1: Be open to meet the Divine anywhere, anytime. (Well Lesson #1)

Group 2: Learn to reach beyond what separates us from community and take action to connect (Well Lesson #2)

Allow Participants to Count Off by Twos or Fours. Then ask them to follow the small group leader who is holding their assigned number. Identify the location of each group. (These locations can also be pre-printed on a sheet of paper, photocopied, and distributed to save time.) Participants should then gather into smaller groups in the designated meeting areas.

Note: If the Bible study is large, divide into more groups and reassign alternately the same Well Lessons to each of the additional groups. In this case, possibly more than one group will be reflecting on each of the Well Lessons. If the Bible Study is small, divide into two groups and permit each group to discuss as many of the reflections as each group desires.

Small Group Study
Small Group Leaders
Each group will have one Well Lesson to explore. For each Well Lesson, there are questions and/or related Scripture references to stimulate discussion.
Sharing Insights
After 15 minutes, designate someone to summarize the small group discussion within the large group presentation that follows. The designated person will have three to five minutes to present.

Large Group Presentations
Reconvene the Group. Call the small groups together.

Explain the Procedure. A representative from each of the small groups will share that group's reflections on the Well Lesson assigned. The large group will have an opportunity to comment on reflections after all presentations have been made. Remind participants of the large group to be attentive and jot down notes or significant points on which comments may be made at the designated time

Remind Small Group Representatives of the Time. Each group representative should summarize the group's reflection in less than five minutes. Allow up to five minutes to discuss each group's presentation.

Note: If there are more than three groups, allow each group three minutes to summarize reflections and encourage small group presenters to keep their reflections within the three minutes.

LIFE APPLICATION DISCUSSION*
If time permits, the larger group can then discuss reflections on the Well Words, Well Language and Well Works sections of their workbook.
Introduction
The Life Application section consists of reflections on the Well Words, Well Language, and Well Works assigned in the Student Book. Participants are asked to share which words (Scriptures) personally framed their journey, which language or affirmations they considered to be personally helpful, and what steps that they would personally take to demonstrate the lessons learned. Discussion should also

address the implications for the church as a whole. Ask for other ideas gleaned from the chapter that can effect positive behavioral changes.

Sharing Insights

This discussion should be open-ended and voluntary. The sharing of personal insights or recommendations for church ministry should be encouraged but not required. The group may have much to share. Be mindful of the time and dedicate only 15 minutes to this exercise.

*Answers are not provided for this section of the study because of the personal or specific nature of the reflections.

Preparation For Next Meeting

Assignment. Participants are asked to read Chapter 3, "A Woman In Time." Review the Well Lessons in preparation for the next session. Encourage them to come to the next session prepared to share their insights on the content of the next chapter.

The Leader may also want to assign small groups or specific Well Lessons to facilitate next week's meeting time. Remind the class to take time for sabbatical.

CLOSING PRAYER

Form a prayer circle and invite all to pray individually for the ability to become persons who are open to God. Close with a prayer of thanksgiving for the deliverance of God's people.

ANSWERS TO BIBLE STUDY APPLICATION

WELL LESSON #1
Be open to meeting the Divine anywhere, anytime.

"Now he had to go through Samaria" (John 4:4, NIV)

1a. Look up the verses below to determine God's readiness to meet us anywhere.

Jonah 2:1, 10—Jonah prayed to the Lord while in the belly of the fish. He said that God answered him. The Lord commanded the fish to vomit Jonah onto dry land.

1 Samuel 1:11—Hannah was in a depressed state. She wanted very much to have a son. Although she knew that she already had her husband's love, this was not enough. The culture of her time required women to bear children. In her depression, she prayed, vowing to give the child back to God, if she were allowed to bear a son. She conceived and bore a son and called his name Samuel, saying, "Because I have asked him of the Lord."

Exodus 3:2-10—The Lord had seen the suffering of the people of Israel in Egypt. He visited Moses in the desert at Horeb, called the mountain of God. God appeared in the form of a burning bush and told Moses that he had been chosen to go to Pharaoh to bring the Israelites out of Egypt.

1b. Do you think these above mentioned meetings were coincidental or deliberate? Give reasons for your answers. (Answers will vary)

WELL LESSON #2
Learn to reach beyond what separates us from community and take action to reconnect.

2a. Jacob and his brother Esau had been separated because of family problems for many years. In Genesis 32, Jacob prepares to meet/reconnect with his brother. Name several things that he did. *He started to make amends by sending a message of his plan to return home to Esau and of his desire to find favor in Esau's eyes. Then Jacob prayed and was reassured of God's promise of prosperity and fruitfulness. He then planned to give his brother a gift.*

2b. What may have happened if Jacob had chosen to stay separated and not to reconnect with his brother? (Answers will vary)

LIFE APPLICATION
Personal Application

Reflect on times in your life when you were not open to God. Why? What happened to change your attitude? What was the outcome?

Reflect on a time when you were opened to God. What happened? How was this experience different from when you weren't open?

Write a prayer for openness to accept God as *"the unseen conductor of orchestrated events" of our lives.* — *Vashti McKenzie*

WELL WORDS

The following Well Words are offered as encouragement you when you feel that you are unable to give God control of your one-hope situation. Select one Well Word per day or per week. Memorize this Well Word. It is your personal spiritual landmark to help you in your journey.

"Do not conform any longer to the pattern of this world, but be transformed by the renewing of your mind. Then you will be able to test and approve what God's will is—his good, pleasing and perfect will" (Romans 12:2, NIV).

"And without faith it is impossible to please God, because anyone who comes to him must believe that he exists and that he rewards those who earnestly seek him" (Hebrews 11:6, NIV).

"Your attitude should be the same as that of Christ Jesus" (Philippians 2:5, NIV).

"Let the wicked forsake his way and the evil man his thoughts. Let him turn to the Lord, and he will have mercy on him, and to our God, for he will freely pardon. For my thoughts are not your thoughts, neither are your ways my ways, declares the Lord" (Isaiah 55:7-8, NIV).

"So you must also be ready..." (Matthew 24:44, NIV).

"I stand at the door and knock...and if anyone opens...I will come in" (Revelation 3:20).

"As we have the opportunity, let us do good..." (Galatians 6:10, NIV)

"Make the most of every opportunity..." (Colossians 4:5)

WELL SABBATICAL

A sabbatical is spending a daily quiet moment alone with God. In our harried society, taking a pregnant pause can be a challenge. Daily quiet sabbatical moments must always be focused upon the Word of God. It should last five minutes, adding minutes as you go along. If you fall asleep, you really needed the rest!

Locate a quiet place, get into a comfortable position and read Philippians 2:5, NIV: "Your attitude should be the same as that of Christ" or Isaiah 55:7-8, which reminds us that our thoughts are not like God's. You may also read 1 Kings 17 where Isaiah enters with the still, small voice of God. Silence is precious. Be still in the silence. Listen for the God without, and the God within. The Divine is present in every moment and in every place. God rewards those who diligently seek Him (Hebrews 11:6).

Being calm with a chaotic mind is impossible. A disciplined mind begins when you seek to put into it what pleases God. Pray that God will grant you the mind of Christ when you face issues and make decisions. Seeking the mind of Christ requires surrendering to God's will. God's will is contained in God's Word and God will not ask you to do anything inconsistent with the nature and character of the Divine. God's desire is always for our highest good. Be still and release the controls of your life to the Transformer whose mercy endures forever. Imagine yourself surrounded by loving strong arms; relax in the embrace and gently lay your head upon the back of the chair as if you were laying your head upon your mother's breast. Be still and take deep breaths; exhale slowly. When we are under stress we often forget to breathe deeply; hear the air expand your chest and rush through your nostrils. Be still and welcome the calm as you focus on communing with God's Spirit.

WELL LANGUAGE

Let the following affirmations of encouragement also guide you in your journey. Write your favorite on a 3x5 or 5x7 file card with a felt-tip pen in a color you prefer.

1. God will meet me in my ordinary.
2. Anonymous is an unacceptable reality.
3. I am a person open to God.
4. Reach out and people will reach back.
5. I am looking for an unexpected opportunity to advance!

WELL WORKS

The following Well Works are provided to help you take steps to demonstrate your new commitment to live out the lessons learned in this session.

Choose one or more Well Works to do during a day.

Take a meditation break daily. Be still for a change. Shield your eyes from the hot sun. Smell the air whip past you. Feel the sand as it falls over your sandaled feet. Look for the presence of God in your ordinary necessities. Be still and listen to the still, small voice of God.

1. Find three poems written anonymously; acknowledge and celebrate the authors in your own way.
2. Identify a person in your community whose life, achievements, and contributions go unnoticed. Write a thank-you note for all their good works.
3. Speak to a person who exists on the fringes of the community. Invite her / him into your world.
4. Instead of going to your regular restaurant, market, library, movie theater, or video store, go across town or into another neighborhood where you know no one and no one knows you. How do you feel?
5. Have you felt like an anonymous person? Write in your journal about the seasons in your life when you wanted to disappear and disconnect from the community...and did!
6. Have you ever had an experience when you chose to decorate a situation or relationship like wall paper covers a wall rather than take center stage? Write about it in your journal.

Church Ministry Application

- How can you enlist the church in praying for the congregation's openness to God in church concerns?
- How does (or could) your church benefit from having a group similar to the Circle of Love founded by Dr. McKenzie?
- How can you make certain that there are no persons in your congregation living on the fringes of your church community?

A WOMAN
IN TIME

For sessions of 90 minutes or more, use the lesson format for PART ONE and PART TWO.

PART ONE

Opening Prayer - 5 minutes

Scripture - 20 minutes

Chapter Highlights* - 15 minutes

PART TWO

Well Lessons

Small Group - 20 minutes

Large Group - 15 minutes

Life Application* - 10 minutes

Closing Prayer - 5 minutes

*Chapter Highlights and Life Application
  Sections are eliminated in 60-minute
  Sessions

For sessions of less than 90 minutes, the Life Application questions may be assigned as homework.

It may appear like an ordinary day. It may feel like just another trip to the store. It may sound like just another task to complete. On the surface it's just another bus, train, subway ride somewhere. Listen with spiritual ears and look with spiritual eyes beyond (the sand, sun and the constant well necessities) what is happening in your life. —Vashti McKenzie

Lesson Aim

At the end of this Bible study session, participants should be able to: a) understand the distinction between our *kronos* (chronological time) and God's *kairos* (the appointed time); b) realize that our *kronos* times are in the hands of God—God is the Creator of chronology; c) recognize that just as God determined a *kairos* moment for the Samaritan woman, God also determines the *kairos* moments of our lives; d) commit to seeking spiritual direction, to be able to recognize the *kairos* moments in which God breaks into our every-day situations; e) give thanks for all of the times when God has arrived at our wells of necessity, just in time.

"...It was about the sixth hour" (John 4:6b, NIV).

PART ONE

OPENING PRAYER – 5 Minutes

Open the session with a prayer of thanksgiving for the Disciplines of the Well and the varied Well Sabbaticals that the participants will experience in this study. Pray that God will bless each participant to:

- Take the time to recognize the *kairos* moments that have occurred in their lives
- Understand the importance of *kairos* moments to Christian living.
- Appreciate God for always having met them at their well of necessity - just in time.
- Trust God's determination of *kairos* moments in their lives.

SCRIPTURE SEARCH – 20 minutes

Ask for a volunteer to read John 4:6-7a aloud to the group, while the group reflects on the timing of this woman's well encounter with Jesus. Compare various translations. Ask the following questions:

1. At what time did the woman come to the well?
It was about the sixth hour. (vv. 6b-7a)

2. In what ways was it the wrong time for her to come to the well?
It was noon, in the heat of the day and most women did not gather water at that time. The usual water gathering time was early in the morning or later in the evening when the sun was lower and the heat was not as great.

3. In what ways was it the right time for her to come to the well?
It was the right time because Jesus was there. Jesus had grown tired from His journey and sat down at the well (v. 6a).

4. Make the distinction between our *kronos* (chronological time) and God's *kairos* (the appointed time). Ask, was this a *kronos* or *kairos* moment for the Samaritan woman? How do you know?

Continue the dialogue by asking the group to consider other biblical personalities who experienced *kairos* moments and what they did with their moments. Ask someone to read Genesis 32:22-31. Discuss how Jacob responded to his *kairos* moment when God appeared to him in the form of a man. *Jacob wrestled with God and said, "I will not let you go unless you bless me" (vv. 23-26).* Ask another student to read Acts 9:3-6 and point out how Saul responded to his *kairos* moment when God appeared to him on the road to Damascus. *Saul believed Jesus and spread the good news about Christ. Ask a volunteer to read Genesis 19:12-26. Discuss how Lot's wife did not take advantage of her* kairos *moment when God provided a way for her and Lot to escape from Sodom and Gomorrah.* She looked back in disobedience. *What was the result of her not taking advantage of her* kairos *moment?* She turned into a pillar of salt. *What lessons do you learn from her example?* Answers will vary.

CHAPTER HIGHLIGHTS –
15 Minutes (recommended for 90 minute sessions only)

Using the content of Chapter 3 as background, give a general overview of the chapter. Be sure to include the following topics:

1. Kronos vs. kairos time
2. Living life conscious of the kairos moments
3. Trusting in and waiting on God to determine when our kairos moments should occur; our timing is not God's timing - He knows when to bring about the necessary changes for our lives

PART TWO

BIBLE STUDY APPLICATION
Introduction

The Bible Study Application section contains two Well Lessons that provide an opportunity to examine what the Bible says about how we live our lives in God's timing.

Allow as much time as necessary to encourage free participation and exchange of ideas and insights.

Procedure

Select Small Group Leaders. Ask for volunteers or select two small group leaders and assign each leader a number from 1-2. Ask the small group leaders to write their number on large sheets of white paper so that they can be seen from a distance. (This can also be done beforehand to save time)

Divide into Small Groups. Inform the participants that they will be separated into small groups. Each group will reflect on both Well Lessons and then present their reflections to the larger group at the end of the study period. The following Well Lessons should be assigned to each group:

Group 1: Learn to be in time, not just on time. (Well Lesson #1)

Group 2: Be aware of kairos occasions. (Well Lesson #2)

Allow Participants to Count Off by Twos. Then ask them to follow the small group leader who is holding their assigned number, 1 or 2. Identify the location of each group. (These locations can also be pre-printed on a sheet of paper, photocopied, and distributed to save time.) Participants should then gather into smaller groups in the designated meeting areas.

Note: If the Bible Study is large, divide into more groups and reassign alternately the same two Well Lessons to each of the additional groups. In this case, possibly more than one group will be reflecting on both of the Well Lessons. If the Bible Study is small, permit one group to reflect on both. Be sure to allow for adequate time to discuss each Well Lesson.

Small Group Study
Small Group Leaders
Each group will have both Well Lessons to explore. For each Well Lesson, there are questions and/or related Scripture references to stimulate discussion.

Sharing Insights
After 20 minutes, designate someone to summarize the small group discussion within the large group presentation that follows. The designated person will have at least five minutes to present.

Large Group Presentations
Reconvene the Group. Call the small groups together.

Explain the Procedure. A representative from each of the small groups will share that group's reflections on the Well Lesson assigned. The large group will be given an opportunity to comment on reflections after all presentations have been made. Remind participants of the large group to be attentive and jot down notes or significant points on which comments may be made at the designated time.

Remind Small Group Presenters of the Time. Each group representative should summarize the group's reflection in at least five minutes. Allow up to five minutes to discuss each group's presentation.

Note: If there are more than two groups, allow each group three minutes to summarize reflections and encourage small group presenters to keep their reflections within the three minutes.

LIFE APPLICATION DISCUSSION*

If time permits, the larger group can then discuss reflections on the Well Words, Well Language and Well Works sections of their workbook.

Introduction

The Life Application sections consist of reflections on the Well Words, Well Language, and Well Works assigned in the Student Book. Participants are asked to share which words and affirmations personally framed their journey and what steps they will personally take to demonstrate the lessons learned. Discussion should also address the implications for the church as a whole.

Sharing Insights

This discussion should be open-ended and voluntary. The sharing of personal insights or recommendations for church ministry should be encouraged but not required. The group may have much to share. Be mindful of the time and dedicate only 10 minutes to this exercise.

*Answers are not provided for this section of the study because of the personal or specific nature of the reflections.

Preparation For Next Meeting

Assignment. Participants are asked to read Chapter 4, "A Woman Pregnant With the Possibilities of God." Review the Well Lessons in preparation for the next session. Encourage them to come to the next session prepared to share their insights on the content of the next chapter.

The Leader may want to assign small groups or specific Well Lessons to facilitate the discussion on the next session.

CLOSING PRAYER

Form a prayer circle and encourage students to reflect on the kairos moments of their lives as the leader gives thanks for all kairos moments realized. Students are then encouraged to reflect on what they can do to further develop a conscience that recognizes kairos moments and takes full advantage of those moments in their lives. The leader will continue to pray for a deepening spiritual life that enables all students to recognize kairos moments.

ANSWERS TO BIBLE STUDY APPLICATION

WELL LESSON #1
Learn to be in time, not just on time.

Being in time means looking beyond the present reality to the unseen hand of God moving behind the scenes.

Read the following Scripture references. How was God moving behind the scenes in the Bible characters' lives?

Joseph (Genesis 37:19-28; 45:1-8)
When Joseph's brothers sold him into slavery, God was preparing Joseph to save his family in the famine.

Ruth and Naomi (Ruth 1:1-5; 4:9-17)
When Ruth and Naomi's husbands died, God was working to produce the line of King David and subsequently the earthly line of Jesus Christ.

The jailer (Acts 16:22-34)
When Paul and Silas were thrown in jail, God was working to save the jailer and his family.

WELL LESSON #2
Be aware of kairos occasions.
Is this the kairos moment to retreat, retrench or move full stream ahead?—Vashti McKenzie

Fill in the missing words from Ecclesiastes 3:1-8. Then review the words in the blanks and discuss why each kairos moment is needed.

There is a time for everything, a season for every activity under heaven: a time to be born and a time to die, a time to plant and a time to uproot, a time to kill and a time to heal, a time to tear down and a time to build, a time to weep and a time to laugh, a time to mourn and a time to dance, a time to scatter stones and a time to gather them, a time to embrace and a time to refrain, a time to search and a time to refrain, a time to search and a time to give up, a time to keep and a time to throw away, a time to tear and a time to mend, a time to be silent and a time to speak, a time to love and a time to hate, a time for war and a time for peace

LIFE APPLICATION
Personal Application
Reflect on the times when God met you at your well of necessity—just in time. List those "in time" situations of your life and write a prayer of thanksgiving to God, for meeting you just in time.

Consider the circumstances when you felt time was running out and you needed an immediate resolution. Consider the times when you prayed for an answer to your problem, or to be met at your well of necessity, only to receive no immediate response:

- You needed to decide on a new job
- You needed to know from where your next paycheck was coming
- You needed to know that you were making the right decision about a relationship (with your wife, husband, or child)

How can remembering that God determines our *kairos* moments help us learn while we wait?

WELL WORDS
The following Well Words are offered as encouragement when you feel that time is running out and become anxious while waiting for God to meet you at your well of necessity. Select one Well Word per day or per week. Memorize this Well Word. It is your personal spiritual landmark to help you in your journey.

"Teach us to number our days aright that we may gain a heart of wisdom" (Psalm 90:12, NIV).

"Be very careful, then, how you live—not as unwise but as wise, making the most of every opportunity, because the days are evil" (Ephesians 5:15-16, NIV).

"But when the time had fully come, God sent his Son, born of a woman, born under law" (Galatians 4:4, NIV).

"Let us not become weary in doing good, for at the proper time we will reap a harvest if we do not give up" (Galatians 6:9, NIV).

"All of the days of my hard service, I will wait for my renewal to come" (Job 14:14b, NIV).

"Wait for the Lord; be strong and take heart and wait for the Lord" (Psalm 27:14, NIV).

WELL SABBATICAL

Take your sabbatical outside if you can. Sit and listen to the silence in a secure place. Smell the silence, hear the silence, and record your thoughts in your travel log or journal. Always remember that you can take your sabbatical on the road. Whenever you come across a space that seems inviting, take a rest and enjoy.

WELL LANGUAGE

Let the following affirmations of encouragement also guide you in your journey. Write your favorite on a 3x5 or 5x7 file card in a felt-tip pen in a color you prefer.

1. In God's time my change will come
2. My times are in the hands of God
3. I will not run ahead of God, but with God
4. What time is it?
5. Don't let this moment pass me by.
6. Hold on, change is coming!

WELL WORKS

The following Well Works are provided to help you take steps to demonstrate new commitment to live out the lessons learned in this session. Choose one or more Well Works to do during a day.

1. Rituals are older than language. They are patterned movements that reflect what you believe. The Lord said to Moses, "Speak to Aaron and say to him, 'When you set up the seven lamps, they are to light the area in front of the lamp stand'" (Numbers 8:1-2, NIV).

We believe that Jesus is the light of the world. We also believe His command to let our light so shine that others may see our good works and Glorify our God in heaven (Matthew 5:16)

2. Tonight, when the house is quiet, play your favorite sacred CD or tape. Light a candle so that the light is thrown forward to remind yourself that those open to God remember to face forward. Tomorrow let the light of Jesus shine through you and take no credit for what God does in or through you.

3. Read one passage of Scripture from Well Words. Enjoy a quiet meditative moment focused upon that Scripture.

4. Ask God, What time is it in your life? Pray that you will become aware of your kairos moments so opportunities won't pass you by. Take advantage of every kairos moment.

5. Record on one side of a 5X7 file card a moment when you thought you were old enough or ready for something, and it didn't happen. Things were not falling into place and you may have become bitter, edgy, or upset by the stall. On the other side, write down when it was your time, when things fell into place because it was your season, your time. Record more of your kairos moments.

6. Place the cards on your collage along with any objects that represent your kairos occasions. For example, dried flowers from a special moment, ticket stubs, photographs, your baby's sock, a wedding invitation, the resume that led to the career you're trained for or wanted, leaves from the tree outside your new home or apartment.

7. Write in your journal about your kairos moments.

Church Ministry Application
Reflect on the kairos moments that have occurred in the life of your local church.
- List the event(s).
- What made the event a kairos or breakthrough moment?
- Do the leadership and laity of your church demonstrate patience in waiting on the Lord? If so, cite examples where the leadership of your church has demonstrated patience. If not, cite those examples.

A WOMAN PREGNANT WITH THE POSSI-BILITIES OF GOD

For sessions of 90 minutes or more, use the lesson format for PART ONE and PART TWO.

PART ONE

Opening Prayer - 5 minutes

Scripture - 20 minutes

Chapter Highlights* - 15 minutes

PART TWO

Well Lessons

Small Group - 20 minutes

Large Group - 15 minutes

Life Application* - 10 minutes

Closing Prayer - 5 minutes

*Chapter Highlights and Life Application Sections are eliminated in 60-minute Sessions

For sessions of less than 90 minutes, the Life Application questions may be assigned as homework.

Living life for and through anyone else but Jesus Christ is an unproductive venture. How can God take you where you have never been before, if you allow someone else to take the journey? It's your life, live it —Vashti McKenzie

Lesson Aim

At the end of this Bible study session, the participants should be able to: a) believe that God has a purpose for their lives; b) assess the consequences of "surrogate living" — letting another individual live out one's life; c) recognize God's purpose for their lives; and d) live it.

"When a Samaritan woman came to draw water, Jesus said to her..." (John 4:7, NIV).

PART ONE

OPENING PRAYER – 5 minutes

Open the session with a prayer of thanksgiving for the Disciplines of the

Well and the varied Well Sabbaticals that the participants will experience in this study. Pray that God will bless each participant to:

- Realize that they are fearfully and wonderfully made - created in the image of God
- Believe that God has a purpose for their lives
- Recognize God's purpose for their lives
- Accept God's purpose for their lives and make a commitment to live it

B. SCRIPTURE SEARCH – 20 Minutes

Preparation: Before class begins, write or type the following numbered statements on a sheet of paper. Then use scissors to separate the statements. (Each statement should be on a separate piece of paper.)

1. I am afraid.
2. I just want to be left alone!
3. I don't believe that I can.
4. If only I could find someone else to do it!
5. I am pregnant with the possibilities of God.
6. I trust God.
7. God has promised me an abundant life.
8. I can do everything through him who gives me strength (Philippians 4:13, NIV).
9. Read Genesis 18:9-10 aloud.
10. Read Genesis 18:14 aloud.

Use a paperclip to keep the statements together until time to distribute them.

Ask someone to read John 4:1-7a aloud to the group. Engage the group in an orchestrated dialogue as you lead in the discussion of the Scripture Distribute all of the printed statements. If there are more than eight volunteers, give two statements to some of the participants.

Inform the class that you will be conducting role-playing exercise. Explain that you will hold up your fingers to indicate when the volunteers are to stand up and read their numbered statements aloud. Encourage volunteers to read their statement and expound further, with feeling.

Begin the dialogue. Reflect on how the Samaritan woman might have felt as she started out on her long, hot journey to the well that day. Had she set out hoping that she would not find anyone there? Do you suppose that she might have real-

45

ly wanted someone else to go to the well that day? What might the Samaritan woman have felt and said?

(Hold up one finger, as volunteer #1 reads the first statement)

Continue in this manner through statement #4.

Or, could the Samaritan woman have said:
(Hold up five fingers, as volunteer #5 reads)

Continue in this manner through statement #8.

Continue the dialogue. Ask volunteers to respond to the following questions: Why was this woman's decision to go to the well, that day, a good one?

What possibilities did she now have that she wouldn't have had had she stayed away from the well?

Open the discussion to other volunteers to reflect on ways in which her story parallels their story. Has anyone ever had to face a difficult situation and really wanted someone else to go in his or her place? What did she or he do? *Confront the situation? Run from the situation?* If she or he sent someone else, why? If he or she didn't send someone else, why not? Point out the importance of confronting all situations in faith; believing that with God, nothing is impossible (Luke 1:37, paraphrased).

Continue the dialogue. In Genesis 18:1-15, three men, sent by the Lord, visit Abraham. He was told that even at their old age, he and his wife, Sarah, would have a son.

(Hold up nine fingers, as volunteer #9 reads the Scripture passage)

Continue in this manner through statement #10.

Conclude the dialogue. Remind the participants that there is nothing impossible for God. Christians should live each day in anticipation of all of God's new possibilities for their lives.

CHAPTER HIGHLIGHTS –
15 Minutes (recommended for 90-minute sessions only)

Using the content of Chapter 4 as background, give a general overview of the chapter. Be sure to include the following topics:

1. Surrogate living and its effects on your life
2. Living life pregnant with the possibilities of God
3. Live life for and through Christ

PART TWO

BIBLE STUDY APPLICATION

Introduction

The Bible Study Application section contains three Well Lessons that provide an opportunity to examine what the Bible says about how we can live our lives filled with the possibilities of God. Allow as much time as necessary to encourage free participation and exchange of ideas and insights.

Procedure

Select Small Group Leaders. Ask for volunteers or select three small group leaders and assign each leader a number from 1-3. Ask the small group leaders to write their number on large sheets of white paper so that they can be seen from a distance. (This can also be done beforehand to save time.)

Divide into Small Groups. Inform the participants that they will be separated into small groups. Each group will reflect on a different Well Lesson and then present their reflections to the larger group at the end of the study period. The Well Lessons should be assigned as follows:

Group 1: Living life for and through anyone else but Jesus Christ is an unproductive venture.

Group 2: Be receptive to the possibilities of God.

Group 3: God is the support beyond our human limitations.

Allow Participants to Count off by Threes. Then ask them to follow the small group leader who is holding their assigned number. Identify the location of each group. (These locations can also be pre-printed on a sheet of paper, photocopied, and distributed to save time.) Participants should then gather into smaller groups in the designated meeting areas.

Note: If the Bible Study is large, divide into more groups and reassign alternately the same three Well Lessons to each of the additional groups. In this case, possibly more than one group will be reflecting on each of the Well Lessons. If the Bible Study is small, divide into two groups and permit each group to discuss as many of the reflections as desired. You may also want to include Well Lesson 3 as part of the homework assignment.

Small Group Study
Small Group Leaders
Each group will have one topic to explore. For each topic, there are questions and/or related Scripture references to stimulate discussion.
Sharing Insights
After 20 minutes, designate someone to summarize the small group discussion in the large group presentation. Remind the designated person that she or he will have only five minutes to present.

Large Group Presentations
Reconvene the Group. Invite all small groups together.

Explain the Procedure. A representative from each of the small groups will share the group's reflections on the Bible Study Application questions with the larger group.

Remind Small Group Representatives of the Time. Each small group presenter should try to summarize the group's discussion in less than five minutes. Allow up to five minutes to discuss each group's presentation.

LIFE APPLICATION DISCUSSION*
If time permits, the larger group can then discuss reflections on the Well Words, Well Language, and Well Works sections of their workbook.
Introduction
The Life Application section contains reflections on the Well Words, Well Language, and Well Works assigned in the Student Book. Participants are asked to share which words and affirmations personally framed their journey and what steps they will personally take to demonstrate the lessons learned. Discussion should also address the implications for the church as a whole.
Sharing Insights
This discussion should be open-ended and voluntary. Sharing personal insights or recommendations for church ministry should be encouraged but not required.

The group may have much to share. Be mindful of the time and dedicate only ten minutes to this exercise.

*Answers are not provided for this section of the study because of the personal or specific nature of the reflections.

Preparation For Next Meeting

Assignment. Participants are asked to read Chapter 5, "A Woman Breaking Down Barriers." Review the Well Lessons in preparation for the next session. Encourage them to come to the next session prepared to share their insights on the content of the next chapter.

The Leader may also want to assign small groups or specific Well Lessons to facilitate next session's meeting time.

CLOSING PRAYER

Form a payer circle and ask for specific prayer requests. Then ask several volunteers to pray, keeping the prayer requests in mind.

ANSWERS TO BIBLE STUDY APPLICATION

WELL LESSON #1
Living life for and through anyone else but Jesus Christ is an unproductive venture.

How can God take you where you have never been before if you allow someone else to take the journey? ... The Bible, God's Standard Operating Procedure Manual, gives the standard operating procedures for life.
— *Vashti McKenzie*

1. Look up the following verses to determine what God's Word says about you. Then assess why living life for or through any human surrogate is unproductive:

Genesis 1:26-7; 9:6 and 5:1—You are created in the image of God.

Psalm 139:14-16—You are fearfully and wonderfully made. God created you uniquely, taking time, love and care to shape and mold me into what I am.

Genesis 2:19,20; Colossians 3:10—God gave you a mind, intellect and knowledge in the image of God, the Creator.

Isaiah 43:7; Psalm 100:3; Ephesians 2:10—You were created by God, for God's glory. As God's Creation and people, our sole purpose is to serve and follow Him.

Galatians 3:28; Ephesians 2:14,15—You are made equal and complete in Jesus Christ. Through Christ, barriers of hostility, prejudice and division are broken down and we are united as one.

John 10:10—You can have an abundant life through your personal acceptance of Jesus Christ as Lord.

2. What benefits do you receive when you believe and live what God's Word says to you?

Isaiah 55:10-11; 2—The assurance that God's Word will not *return empty*: be assured that you can rely on God's Word to accomplish the purpose for which God sent it.

2 Timothy 3:16-17—All Scripture is *God-breathed* and is useful for teaching, rebuking, correcting and training in righteousness *so that the man of God may be thoroughly equipped* for every good work.

Psalm 12:6; 18:30—The assurance that God's Word is trustworthy because *God's Word is flawless; God's Word is perfect.*

1 Samuel 3:21—The assurance that God will reveal Himself through His Word.

James 1:22-25; I John 2:5 - The assurance that God's Word will *bless you. Obedience* to *God's Word results in* God's love being made complete in you.

WELL LESSON #2
Be Receptive to the Possibilities of God.

The world often views impossible, the possibilities of God. We must learn to be receptive and to not accept the limitations that the world may place on our lives. Think on God's purpose for your life and pray for the Holy Spirit to guide you towards reaching that greater creative divine possibility.

Match the identities of persons who were receptive to the possibilities of God that the world had thought impossible, with the blessing that God granted them.

Esther (Esther 5-7)	a. Believed God and saved her people
Jairus (Mark 5:21-43)	b. Believed God for the resurrection of his daughter
Abraham (Genesis 15:6)	c. Believed God for a son
David (I Samuel 17:32-50)	d. Believed God for a victory against Goliath
Hemorrhaging woman (Luke 8:43-48)	e. Believed God for a healing

WELL LESSON #3
God is the support beyond our human limitations!

Many times we become frustrated in our life's journey, as we attempt to handle the weight of the world by ourselves. We forget that God is able to handle the heavy burdens caused by expanding possibilities and increasing responsibilities in our lives. In fact, God calls us to "cast thy burden upon the Lord ..." and God further says that "he shall sustain thee: he shall never suffer the righteous to be moved" (Psalm 55:22, KJV).

Using the verses below, review the answers to these basic questions regarding God's divine support. Discuss any new insights you receive.

1. Who is eligible for God's Divine support? (Galatians 3:26-29; Romans 8:14)
All are Sons and Daughters of God through faith in Jesus Christ and baptism into Christ. We are all one in Christ, regardless of ethnicity, social standing, or gender. All those being led by the Spirit are sons of God.

2. How much of my heavy burden should I ask God to help me carry? Or, how much of my heavy burden can God handle? (Ephesians 3:20; 2 Chronicles 19:12) **God can handle exceeding and abundantly more than anything we could ask or think - there is no limit to God's power**

3. How do we begin to stretch out on God's strength and power to support us in carrying our heavy life burdens? (Proverbs 3:5-6; James 4:3) **Trust in the Lord and don't lean on your own understanding. Ask for what you need, and pray that your desires are pleasing to the Lord and in accordance with His will for you.**

4. What outcome does God grant to those who trust in Him and accept His divine purpose for their lives? (Romans 8:28; Psalm 30:5) **God will work all things for the good. Difficulties may come, but joy will come in the morning.**

LIFE APPLICATION
Personal Application
Reflect on how faithful you have been with living out the possibilities of God. Have you always lived out God's purposes in your life? Or have you ignored, rejected, and denied the possibilities of God? What caused you to not fulfill the possibilities of God in your life?
- Fear
- Little Courage
- Little Faith
- Low Self-esteem

Determine what caused you to ignore, reject or deny those possibilities and ask God to bring healing and restoration to your life.

WELL WORDS
Select one Well Word per day or per week. Memorize this Well Word. It is your personal spiritual landmark to help you in your journey.

"Blessed is she who has believed that what the Lord has said to her will be accomplished" (Luke 1:45, NIV).

"We have this treasure in jars of clay to show that this all-surpassing power is from God and not from us." (2 Corinthians 4:7, NIV).

"...Woman, you have great faith! Your request is granted" (Matthew 15:28, NIV).

"...Come with me by yourselves to a quiet place and get some rest" (Mark 6:31, NIV).

"As a mother comforts her child, so will I comfort you; and you will be comforted ..." (Isaiah 66:13, NIV).

"...I have come that they may have life, and have it to the full." (John 10:10, NIV)

"I praise you because I am fearfully and wonderfully made..." (Psalm 139:14, NIV)

"...Put on the new self, which is being renewed in knowledge in the image of its Creator." (Colossians 3:10, NIV)

"You have been given fullness in Christ, who is the head over every power and authority." (Colossians 2:10, NIV)

WELL SABBATICAL

Spend quiet moments meditating upon Luke 1:37, NIV: "For nothing is impossible with God."

What impossible problems, fears and doubts, deny God's possibility for you? Write about it in your journal.

WELL LANGUAGE

Let the following affirmations of encouragement also guide you in your journey. Write your favorite on a 3x5 or 5x7 file card in a felt-tip pen in a color you prefer.

1. I am pregnant with the possibilities of God.
2. God is able to handle the weight.
3. I am stretching out on the word of God.
4. I can birth new ideas, new dreams, new visions and new realities.
5. When shall we live if not now?
6. If there is no enemy within, the enemy outside can do us no harm.

WELL WORKS

The following Well Works are provided to help you take steps to demonstrate your new commitment to live out the lessons learned in this session:

1. Take a spiritual vitamin daily. A spiritual vitamin is taken by looking up and reading the Scriptures cited in this chapter and others from the Word of God.

2. Purchase a devotional, if you haven't already. Read it daily, perhaps during your sabbatical, to help you dwell on the pure, lovely, honorable, just, and true.

3. Identify one verse that elicits a warm response in you. A verse that makes you smile, encourages your heart, or makes you feel good can become your unbiblical cord that nourishes the new life growing in you.

4. In a color you love write on a 5x7 index card: God is able to carry the weight! Put it on your dresser or bathroom mirror, refrigerator door, or some place where you will see it every day.

5. Work on your collage. Identify those images that represent new possibilities for you. Remember to make room for the new arrival since you are pregnant with the possibilities of God. You could get balloons in a color you absolutely adore representing areas of concern in your life—home, career, spouse, relationships, parents, in-laws, and mental and physical health. Stretch the balloons by blowing them up to indicate your expanding capability that God is helping to handle. Write on the balloon what changes you are praying for. Attach the balloon(s) to your collage, taking care not to break the balloons!

6. Write in your journal the new ideas God is birthing in you.

Church Ministry Application

Reflect on the ways that your local church has limited the possibilities of God in the following areas:

- In the surrounding neighborhood
- In the spiritual teachings
- In the educational goals
- What has prevented your church from aspiring to new possibilities?
- What kinds of activities do you suggest to inspire God's "possibility" thinking among the membership?

A WOMAN BREAKING DOWN BARRIERS

For sessions of 90 minutes or more, use the lesson format for PART ONE and PART TWO.

PART ONE
Opening Prayer - 5 minutes
Scripture - 15 minutes
Chapter Highlights* - 20 minutes

PART TWO
Well Lessons
Small Group - 15 minutes
Large Group - 20 minutes
Life Application* - 10 minutes
Closing Prayer - 5 minutes
*Chapter Highlights and Life Application
  Sections are eliminated in 60-minute
  Sessions

For sessions of less than 90 minutes, the Life Application questions may be assigned as homework.

The Samaritan woman narrows her eyes in the glare of the sun seeing this man leaning against the wall of the well. She had no idea that it was Jesus of Nazareth who was always doing the unexpected. There are times in the history of our lives when Jesus, in His wise providence, does the very things we least expect.
— Vashti McKenzie

Lesson Aim
At the end of this Bible study session, the participants should be able to: a) reflect on the walls and boundaries that exist in their lives; b) realize that Jesus came to break through all walls and boundaries that divide and threaten to overcome us; and c) learn to expect God to break through when we least expect it!

The Samaritan woman said to him, "You are a Jew and I am a Samaritan woman. How can you ask me for a drink?" (John 4:9, NIV).

PART ONE

OPENING PRAYER – 5 Minutes

Open the session with a prayer of thanksgiving for the Disciplines of the Well and the varied Well Sabbaticals that the participants will experience in this study. Pray that God will bless each participant to:

- Focus on how fearfully and wonderfully he or she is made in the image of God.
- Recognize that Jesus breaks through our many walls and boundaries when we least expect it.
- Celebrate and rejoice in the times when Jesus unexpectedly touched her or his life and a breakthrough occurred.

SCRIPTURE SEARCH – 15 Minutes

Ask a volunteer to read John 4:7-9 aloud to the group and others to answer the following questions:

1. When Jesus asked the Samaritan woman for a drink, Jesus did the "unexpected" according to Jewish tradition. Why was Jesus' action so "unexpected"?
According to the Jewish patriarchal society, women were thought to be inferior and as a Jewish man, Jesus was prohibited from speaking to her. Jesus' asking this woman for a drink would have been an unsanctioned and "unexpected" action. (v. 7b)

Also Jesus was a Jew and Jews were not permitted to speak to Samaritans. (v. 9)

2. What two barriers or walls did Jesus break through when He decided to speak to the woman?
Jesus broke through the gender and race barriers that existed.

3. Do such gender and race barriers still exist today? List examples of these barriers and continue to dialogue. **(Answers may vary)**

4. Do such gender and race barriers exist within our churches today? List examples and continue to dialogue. **(Answers may vary)**

CHAPTER HIGHLIGHTS –
20 minutes (recommended for 90-minute sessions only)

Using the content of Chapter 5 as background, give a general overview of the chapter. Be sure to include the following topics:

1. Jesus, in His wise providence, does the very thing we least expect
2. Jesus observes no petty distinctions of race and gender
3. God specializes in breakthroughs
4. Extend beyond self to reach others

Bible Background: The Samaritan Woman needed a Breakthrough

It is important to note the Samaritan woman needed a breakthrough. For some time, she and many others were living as inferior beings because of their race and gender. Jesus' encounter with her when she least expected it provided a breakthrough for not only the Samaritan woman, but many others. Ask the class to respond to the following question:

1. What were the barriers that were standing in the way of her breakthrough? Participants should mention the following in their responses:
- **She was a woman (4:7a)**
- **The role of women in ancient Palestine:**
- **The Hebrew woman's importance is tied to her ability to bear children or her marital status**
- **Women are considered property of men; either husbands or fathers**
- **Women are listed among the properties that one should not covet (Exodus 20:17)**
- **She was a Samaritan and Jews did not associate with Samaritans (4:9)**

2. What evidence do we have that this woman's breakthrough created a breakthrough for others?
In John 4: 28-30, Scripture records that after the woman received her breakthrough, she left her water pot and went into the city and told others to "Come, see a Man." (4:29). They followed her out of the city to him.

Ask volunteers to read the following Scriptures that record breakthroughs and reflect on how Jesus does the "unexpected." Point out what barriers Jesus broke through to touch the lives of these people.

John 8:1-11 - The woman caught in adultery sees a breakthrough as Jesus challenges her accusers and tells her to go and sin no more (vv. 7-11)

Luke 23:40-43 - The thief who hanged on the cross with Jesus received his breakthrough, even upon his impending death, as he asked to be remembered when Jesus came into His kingdom.

Mark 1:40-44 - A leprous man considered ceremonially unclean and an outcast was healed. Jesus broke through this stigma, touched and healed him.

PART TWO

BIBLE STUDY APPLICATION
Introduction

The Bible Study Application section contains three Well Lessons that provide insights to principles for breakthrough living that can be applied daily. Each Well Lesson will also explore what the Bible says about breakthrough situations. Allow as much time as necessary to encourage free participation and exchange of ideas and insights.

Procedure

Select Small Group Leaders. Ask for volunteers or select three small group leaders and assign each leader a number from 1-3. Ask the small group leaders to write their number on large sheets of white paper so that they can be seen from a distance. (This can also be done beforehand to save time).

Divide into Small Groups. Inform the participants that they will be separated into small groups. Each group will reflect on a different Well Lesson and then present their reflections to the larger group at the end of the study period. The Well Lessons should be assigned as follows:

Group 1: God does not recognize the petty distinctions of race and gender that divide kingdoms and communities. (Well Lesson #1)

Group 2: Learn to move forward even without the help of others. (Well Lesson #2)

Group 3: Apply God's grace and inclusion to every situation and let your higher self break down barriers. (Well Lesson #3)

Allow Participants to Count off by Threes. Then ask them to follow the small group leader who is holding their assigned number. Identify the location of each group. (These locations can also be pre-printed on a sheet of paper, photocopied, and distributed to save time). Participants should then gather into smaller groups in the designated meeting areas.

Note: If the Bible Study is large, divide into more groups and reassign alternately the same three Well Lessons to each of the additional groups. In this case, possibly more than one group will be reflecting on each of the Well Lessons. If the Bible Study is small, divide into two groups and permit each group to discuss as many of the reflections as each group desires. You may also want to include Well Lesson 3 as part of the homework assignment.

Small Group Study

Small Group Leaders

Each group will have one Well Lesson to explore. For each Well Lesson, here are questions and/or related Scripture references to stimulate discussion.

Sharing Insights

After 15 minutes, designate someone to summarize the small group discussion within the large group presentation that follows. The designated person will have five minutes to present.

Large Group Presentations

Reconvene the Group. Call the small groups together.

Explain the Procedure. A representative from each of the small groups will share that group's reflections on the Well Lesson assigned. The large group will be given an opportunity to comment on reflections after all presentations have been made. Remind participants of the large group to be attentive and jot down notes or significant points on which comments may be made at the designated time.

Remind Small Group Representatives of the Time. Each group representative should summarize the group's reflection in less than five minutes. Allow up to five minutes to discuss each group's presentation.

Note: If there were more than three groups, allow each group three minutes to summarize reflections and encourage small group presenters to keep their reflections within the three minutes.

LIFE APPLICATION DISCUSSION*

If time permits, the larger group can discuss reflections on the Well Words, Well Language, and Well Works sections of their workbook.

Introduction

The Life Application section consists of reflections on the Well Words, Well Language, and Well Works assigned in the Student Book. Participants are asked to share which words and affirmations personally framed their journey and what steps they will personally take to demonstrate the lessons learned. Discussion should also address the implications for the church as a whole.

Sharing Insights

This discussion should be open-ended and voluntary. Sharing personal insights or recommendations for church ministry should be encouraged but not required. The group may have much to share. Be mindful of the time and dedicate only 10 minutes to this exercise.

*Answers are not provided for this section of the study because of the personal or specific nature of the reflections.

Preparation For Next Meeting

Assignment. Participants are asked to read Chapter 6, "A Woman Overcomes Learned Ignorance." Review the Well Lessons in preparation for the next session. Encourage participants to come to the next session prepared to share their insights on the contents of the next chapter.

CLOSING PRAYER

Ask students to go back to their small Bible study groups and form small prayer circles. Invite individuals within groups to give a sentence prayer of thanksgiving for a breakthrough experienced or a breakthrough that she or he is asking God to provide. Take three to five minutes for this prayer circle. Leader will then close this prayer time with a prayer of thanksgiving for the deliverance of God's people.

ANSWERS TO BIBLE STUDY APPLICATION

WELL LESSON #1

Petty distinctions of race and gender are not valid in the eyes of God.

Realize that the petty distinctions of race and gender, that are used to divide kingdoms and communities, are no longer valid in the eyesight of God.
— *Vashti McKenzie*

1. Look up the verses below to examine what God says about the petty distinctions that divide us.

Galatians 3:28
We are neither Greek nor Jew: bond nor free; male nor female; we are all one in Christ Jesus.

Romans 3:22-23
The righteousness of God is to all and on all who believe and have faith in Jesus Christ. There is no difference because all have sinned and fall short of God's glory - no one is more righteous than another.

Ephesians 2:14
Jesus, Himself, broke down the middle wall of separation —which was the wall in the temple that had previously separated the Gentiles from the Jews.

Colossians 3:11
In putting on the new man and becoming more like Christ, we take on a renewed knowledge and no longer hold on to the barriers that separated us: "there is neither Greek nor Jew, circumcised nor uncircumcised, barbarian, Scythian, slave nor free, but Christ is all and in all" (v.11, NKJV)

2. Jesus demonstrated that petty differences and barriers could be broken in very physical and tangible ways. Remember that, like Jesus, we too must demonstrate that petty differences and barriers are not valid by taking some physical and tangible actions. Match Jesus' action with the Scripture reference that names a barrier.

a. John 4:7b   Jesus *spoke* to a Samaritan woman
b. Luke 5:12-16   Jesus *touched* a leper
c. Luke 7:36-39   Jesus *made Himself available* to a sinner
                      who anoints His feet

WELL LESSON #2
Learn to move forward even without the help of others.

Jesus spoke through tradition, culture, gender and law to affirm the Samaritan woman. He validated her personhood. — Vashti McKenzie

Jesus helped the Samaritan woman despite what the other Jews, disciples, or the societal, historical leaders had to say. Jesus did not care what they thought.
Use the verses below to answer the following questions:

1. Where were the disciples when Jesus spoke to the woman?
The disciples had gone into the city to buy food (4:8)

2. What was their reaction to Jesus' talking to this woman?
They marveled that Jesus had talked with a woman (4:27)

3. Did they confront Jesus about her?
No, no one asked Jesus about the woman (4:27)

4. List reasons why they might not have confronted Jesus about the woman.
They trusted that Jesus knew what He was doing.

They didn't understand but were accustomed to Jesus operating outside of their understanding - they were getting used to his "unexpected" actions.

They hoped to have an opportunity to ask Jesus later about what had occurred.

They witnessed the expression on her face, realized that something extraordinary had just occurred, and were standing in awe and anticipation to hear more.

5. Realize that many times when you are called to go beyond yourself to break through barriers, you may face criticism and unpopularity. You must still go forward and trust God to give you the courage and power to face and break through barriers and obstacles in life.

6. Look up the verses below and explain how they can motivate you to continue doing what is right in the sight of the Lord and to move forward, despite possible criticism from the world.

Proverbs 21:3
Doing what is right and just is more acceptable to the Lord than sacrifice.

Luke 16:15
Justifying yourself among men is an abomination in the sight of God. He knows our hearts and we must seek to be justified before God - do what pleases Him!

1 Samuel 16:7
The Lord does not see as man sees; for man looks at the outward appearance and the Lord looks at the heart.

WELL LESSON #3
Apply God's grace and inclusion to every situation and let your higher self break down barriers.

It is important to note that Jesus' decision to break through the barriers of race and gender and speak to the woman at the well, prepared the way for the woman to be an agent of change for a whole community. Just as this breaking down barriers made way for the salvation of an entire Samaritan community, our breaking down barriers can also bring the good news to a broken generation and community.

Look up the following Scriptures that remind us that we are to let God's Holy Spirit help us to break down barriers and reach others.

Matthew 28:19-20, NKJV
Go and make disciples of all nations.

Mark 16:15, NKJV
Go into all the world and preach the gospel to every creature.

Matthew 28:37-40
We are called to serve the "least of these."

LIFE APPLICATION
Personal Application

You wonder if the Samaritan woman articulated her frustrations as a victim of her time. Did she live with silent resignation? Did she share her frustrations of denied personhood and rejected womanhood with anyone?
— *Vashti McKenzie*

Reflect on the barriers that you have allowed to stand as obstacles in your life. Many of us are frustrated because we have accepted the boundaries, barriers, or walls that society, family members, or others have placed on our lives.

Have you considered why those barriers have remained in your life and prevented your breakthrough? We must remember to turn to Jesus, be willing to make changes, and allow Jesus to break through our broken places.

WELL WORDS

The following Well Words are offered as encouragement when you feel that you are having difficulty expecting a breakthrough in your life. Select one Well Word each day or each week. Memorize this Well Word. It is your personal spiritual landmark to help you in your journey.

"To do what is right and just is more acceptable to the Lord than sacrifice" (Proverbs 21:3, NIV).

"... who shows no partiality to princes and does not favor the rich over the poor, for they are all the work of his hands?" (Job 34:19, NIV).

"Then Peter began to speak: 'I now realize how true it is that God does not show favoritism'" (Acts 10:34, NIV).

"There is no difference between Jew and Gentile — the same Lord is Lord of all and richly blesses all who call on him" (Romans 10:12, NIV).

"Defend the cause of the weak and fatherless; maintain the rights of the poor and oppressed" (Psalm 82:3, NIV).

WELL SABBATICAL

In your quiet time, meditate on two Scriptures: Psalm 139 and Galatians 3:28.

Be still. Focus your thoughts on how fearfully and wonderfully you are made in the image of God.

Pray this prayer: "My God, I come to you today knowing that I was intentionally created. If anyone makes the mistake of excluding me, Jesus, help me to be confident in the truth that You have already included me. For I know that You will never leave me or forsake me. In Jesus' name."

WELL LANGUAGE

Let the following affirmations of encouragement also guide you in your journey. Write your favorite on a 3x5 or 5x7 file card in a felt-tip pen in a color you prefer.

1. My uniqueness does not mean I am inferior or superior. It means I am unique.
2. Look for the best in everyone.
3. Do not exclude what God includes.
4. My freedom does not require the enslavement of another human.
5. I will not allow other people's prejudices to create obstacles for me.
6. I am loved. I am wanted. I belong (place hand over heart and repeat).

WELL WORKS

The following Well Works are provided to help you take steps to demonstrate your commitment to live out the lessons learned in this session:

Read biographies of women from cultures other than your own

Study a culture different from your own

Learn to say a few words or phrases from a language not native to your heritage or country of origin

Rent a video such as Schindler's List, Amistad, Philadelphia, West Side Story or Shogun. Put yourself in the shoes of those who were excluded. How do you think it felt? How would you behave differently?

Church Ministry Application

Do gender and race barriers exist within your local church? Describe those barriers. What is being done to break down those barriers? What programs exist within your church to encourage ministry beyond its physical walls?

- Ministry to the neighborhood?
- Ministry around the globe?
- Ministry to the unchurched?
- Suggest ideas for programs that your church might institute to help members extend beyond the ordinary to reach others.

A WOMAN OVER-COMES LEARNED IGNORANCE

For sessions of 90 minutes or more, use the lesson format for PART ONE and PART TWO.

PART ONE
Opening Prayer - 5 minutes
Scripture - 15 minutes
Chapter Highlights* - 20 minutes

PART TWO
Well Lessons
Small Group - 15 minutes
Large Group - 20 minutes
Life Application* - 10 minutes
Closing Prayer - 5 minutes
*Chapter Highlights and Life Application
   Sections are eliminated in 60-minute
   Sessions

For sessions of less than 90 minutes, the Life Application questions may be assigned as homework.

Lesson Aim

At the end of this Bible study session, participants should be able to: a) define learned ignorance and learned helplessness; b) list how these behaviors can prevent them from living their lives to the fullest; c) understand that through Christ they are given the power to accomplish great things; d) confidently seek the boldness to learn and act upon all knowledge that is given in Christ.

"Jesus answered her, 'If you knew the gift of God and who it is that asks you for a drink, you would have asked him and he would have given you living water" (John 4:10, NIV).

PART ONE

OPENING PRAYER - 5 Minutes

Open the session with a prayer of thanksgiving to the Lord for the Disciplines of the Well and the varied Well Sabbaticals that the participants will experience in this study. Pray that

God will bless each participant to:
- Understand some of the reasons why learned ignorance and learned help-lessness are practiced
- Recognize the limitations placed on their lives through practicing learned ignorance or learned helplessness
- Believe and receive God's plan for their life
- Be confident that according to Philippians 4:13, they can "do all things through Christ who gives us strength."

SCRIPTURE SEARCH – 15 Minutes

Ask someone to read John 4:7-10 aloud and ask others to answer the following questions:

1. Jesus, tired from His journey, sat down at the well when a Samaritan woman came to draw water. What did Jesus ask her?
Jesus asked her for a drink.

2. What response did the Samaritan woman give to Jesus?
You are a Jew and I am a Samaritan Woman. How can you ask me for a drink?

3. Why did she respond in this way?
The Jews did not associate with Samaritans.

4. How did Jesus respond to her observation?
Jesus told her that if she knew the gift of God and who it is that asks her for a drink, she would have asked him and he would have given her living water.

Ask for volunteers to look up the following Scriptures to explore what the Bible, God's written Word, says about the gift of God:

Romans 6:23 - *The gift of God is eternal life in Christ Jesus our Lord.*

Ephesians 2:8-9 - *Salvation is a gift of God that comes by grace, through faith - and not by our works.*

John 3:16 - *God loved the world so much that He gave his only son - the gift of God!*

Acts 2:38 - *The Holy Spirit is a gift of God that is made available to those who repent and are baptized.*

CHAPTER HIGHLIGHTS –
20 Minutes (recommended for 90-minute sessions only)

Using the content of Chapter 6 as background, give a general overview of the chapter. Be sure to include the following topics:

1. Definitions of "learned ignorance" and "learned helplessness"
2. How do learned ignorance and helplessness occur in our lives?
3. Jesus seeks to acquaint us with the gift of God.

PART TWO

BIBLE STUDY APPLICATION
Introduction

The Bible Study Application section contains three Well Lessons that provide an opportunity to examine what the Bible says about learned ignorance and how we can overcome this practice in our lives. The discussion of the Well Lessons should confirm that the students understand the basic principles of living beyond learned ignorance. Allow as much time as necessary to encourage free participation and exchange of ideas and insights.

Procedure

Select Small Group Leaders. Ask for volunteers or select three small group leaders and assign a number to each leader. Ask the small group leaders to write their numbers on large sheets of white paper so that they can be seen from a distance. (This can also be done beforehand to save time).

Divide into Small Groups. Inform the participants that they will be separated into three groups. Each group will study a different Well Lesson and then present their reflections to the larger group at the end of the study period. The Well Lessons should be assigned as follows:

Group 1: You're not just a deliverer; you can give birth to new ideas.
Group 2: You must take risks.
Group 3: The challenge to change is up to you.

Allow Participants to Count Off by Threes. Then ask them to follow the small group leader who is holding their assigned number. Identify the location of each group. (These locations can also be pre-printed on a sheet of paper, photocopied, and distributed to save time.) Participants should then gather into smaller groups in the designated meeting areas.

Small Group Study
Small Group Leaders
Each group will have one Well Lesson to explore. For each Well Lesson, there are questions and/or related Scripture references to stimulate discussion.
Sharing Insights
After 15 minutes, designate someone to summarize the small group discussion within the large group presentation that follows. The designated person will have five minutes to present.

Large Group Presentations
Reconvene the Group. Call the small groups together.

Explain the Procedure. A representative from each of the small groups will share that group's reflections on the Well Lesson assigned. The large group will have an opportunity to comment on reflections after all presentations have been made. Remind participants of the large group to be attentive and jot down notes or significant points on which comments may be made at the designated time.

Remind Small Group Representatives of the Time. Each group representative should summarize the group's reflection in less than five minutes. Allow up to five minutes to discuss each group's presentation.

LIFE APPLICATION DISCUSSION*
If time permits, the larger group can then discuss reflections on the Well Words, Well Language and Well Works sections of their workbook.
Introduction
The Life Application section consists of reflections on the Well Words, Well Language, and Well Works assigned in the Student Book. Participants are asked to share which words personally framed their journey and what steps they will personally take to demonstrate the lessons learned. Discussion should also address the implications for the church as a whole.
Sharing Insights
That discussion should be open-ended and voluntary. The sharing of personal

insights or recommendations for church ministry should be encouraged but not required. The group may have much to share. Be mindful of the time and dedicate only 10 minutes to this exercise.

*Answers are not provided for this section of the study because of the personal or specific nature of the reflections.

Preparation For Next Meeting

Assignment. Participants are asked to read Chapter 7, "Woman Discovers a New Way of Thinking." Review the Well Lessons in preparation for the next session. Encourage them to come to the next session prepared to share their insights on the content of the next chapter.

The Leader may also want to assign small groups or specific Well Lessons to facilitate next week's meeting time.

CLOSING PRAYER

Form a prayer circle and invite all to pray individually for the confidence to accept the gift of God in their lives and the boldness to act on that gift.

ANSWERS TO BIBLE STUDY APPLICATION

WELL LESSON #1
You're not just a deliverer, you can give birth to new ideas.

Jesus said to the Samaritan woman, If you knew what I had and who I was, your behavior would be different. You would be asking me for water. — Vashti McKenzie

"Jesus answered her, 'If you knew the gift of God and who it is that asks you for a drink, you would have asked him and he would have given you living water" (John 4:10, NIV).

There are many within our community, who practice learned ignorance and decide not to give birth, including those who choose to:
1. Make a deliberate decision "not to know"
2. Be unresponsive
3. Not avail themselves of knowledge and information
4. Intentionally ignore invitations and opportunities
5. Refuse accountability and responsibility

For most people, learned ignorance does not occur suddenly, but it is a developed attitude resulting from repeated failures in their lives. For the Samaritan woman, her repeated failures - marriage, acceptance within her community, belief in herself - resulted in not knowing Jesus and what He could make available to her. The possibility of meeting Jesus, the Redeemer, probably never entered her mind!

1. The following Scripture references point to other Bible personalities who had not thought about giving birth to new possibilities, but Jesus changed things. Look up the verses below and describe how Jesus changed their point of views and helped them to give birth.

John 5:5-15
The man at the pool of Bethesda had suffered an infirmity for 38 years and had been lying by the pool, helplessly, waiting for the moving of the waters and for someone to put him into the pool. He was so preoccupied with his condition that he did not know who Jesus was and probably never expected deliverance at the pool any time soon. Jesus revealed His healing power as He instructed the man to "Rise, take up your bed and walk" (John 5:8, NKJV).

Luke 24:13-35
Two men on the road to Emmaus were preoccupied with the life and death of Jesus and their failed hope that the now crucified Jesus could have been the one to redeem Israel. As they walked, they spoke in disbelief, of the message that the women had given to them that Jesus was no longer in the tomb. These men, in their preoccupation and disbelief, failed to believe that Jesus was indeed gone from the tomb and also failed to see that the man with whom they spoke was Jesus. Jesus revealed to these men His true identity.

2. Now look up the verses below and describe how the following people faced their failures but did not let those failures prevent them from giving birth, seeing the Lord and experiencing His healing power, grace and mercy.

Mark 5:25-34
The woman with an issue of blood for twelve years, tried many physicians with the hope that they could heal her, but found none to be suc-

cessful. When she heard about Jesus, she made her way to Him and touched His garment. She did not let failed attempts at healing prevent her from experiencing Jesus.

Matthew 9:2-8
A man sick with the palsy was brought to Jesus for healing. Although he was a sinner, he did not let his sinfulness prevent him from being taken to Jesus and seeking His healing power. Jesus acknowledged his faith, forgave him and healed him.

Luke 8:26-36
The Gadarene demoniac who had suffered from demons for a long time and lived in the tombs, saw Jesus and responded to Jesus' casting the demons out of his body. He did not remain hidden in the tombs but came out and met Jesus when He arrived on the Gadarene shore. This man was healed and sat at Jesus' feet.

WELL LESSON #2
You must take risks.
Raise the standard by going beyond your comfort zone into new territory. Taking risks is the enemy of learned ignorance; it builds courage and results in action.

1. Match the following verses with those who were not afraid to take risks. How did each one take risks?

a David	a. 1 Samuel 17:32-37 **David stood up to Goliath**
b Job	b. Job 2:9-10 **Job stood up to his wife and told her he would not curse God.**
c Vashti	c. Esther 1:10-22 **Vashti stood up to the king and refused to be paraded before his princes and servants.**

WELL LESSON #3
The challenge to change is up to you.

1. How can the following Scriptures help change learned ignorance?

Philippians 4:13
I can do everything through him who gives me strength.

Matthew 17:20
If you have faith as small as a mustard seed, you can say to this mountain, 'Move from here to there' and it will move. Nothing will be impossible for you.

2 Timothy 1:7
For God did not give us a spirit of timidity, but a spirit of power, of love and of self-discipline.

Matthew 28:20b
And surely I am with you always, to the very end of the age.

LIFE APPLICATION
Personal Application
Reflect on the times when you have practiced learned ignorance or learned helplessness. Determine what caused you to practice these behaviors. Place a check mark beside the possible cause for this behavior and write your reflections in the space provided.

_____ Was this behavior a result of a developed attitude?

_____ Was this behavior a result of cultural reality? A societal or family practice?

Ask God to give healing and restoration to your life. It is in these moments of reflection that we must remember the Word of God, the promises and assurances that it reveals to us about not surrendering to behaviors of learned ignorance and learned helplessness in our lives.

WELL WORDS
The following Well Words are offered as encouragement when you feel that you are resorting to patterns of learned ignorance or learned helplessness. Select one Well Word per day or per week. Memorize this Well Word. It is your personal spiritual landmark to help you in your journey.

"I can do everything through Him who gives me strength." Philippians 4:13

"Every prudent man acts out of knowledge, but a fool exposes folly."
Proverbs 13:16, NIV

"The sluggard craves and gets nothing, but the desires of the diligent are fully satisfied." Proverbs 13:4, NIV

"...being confident of this, that he who began a good work in you will carry it on to completion until the day of Christ Jesus." Philippians 1:6, NIV

"God is able to do more abundantly than we ask..." Ephesians 3:20, NIV
"Trust in the Lord with all you heart and lean not on your own understanding." Proverbs 3:5-6, NIV

"We are more than Conquerors..." Romans 8:28-29

WELL SABBATICAL

This is an excellent time to begin morning sabbaticals if you haven't already done so. Rise at least thirty minutes to an hour before your usual time. Go to your place of refuge and be still before the Lord. In the early morning silence, before dawn and daily routines, ask God to show you areas of planned ignorance and helplessness within you.

Make a list and trace it to the time when this pattern began, or write about how it has been developed and reinforced by your home life, loved ones, or your own wants and desires.

- Confess and repent.
- Spend several mornings asking God to show you an opportunity to expand your world.
- Look for ways to apply new information. It's possible to see things that everyone sees in a different light during prayer.

WELL LANGUAGE

Write these words on your file cards in a color you simply adore. Place the file cards on your mirror in the bathroom, above your light switches, on the computer-screen saver, bulletin boards, refrigerator doors, or any place you will walk by and see them on a regular basis. Write one word on several cards. Each time you see the card, repeat the word as a prayer for yourself and for others.

1. Confident
2. Capable
3. Courageous
4. Consistent

5. Creative
6. Committed
7. You'll never know until you try.
8. You are equipped for the task.
9. Change is an opportunity to be explored, not feared.
10. I will commit my way to the Lord and the Divine Savior will bring it to pass.
11. Encouragement affirms risk

WELL WORKS

The following Well Works are provided to help you take steps to demonstrate your new commitment to live out the lessons learned in this session:
Choose one or more Well Works to do during a day.

1. "To do" lists have been the tools of time managers for years. Your Well "To do" list should consist of those things you do not know and need to know in your spiritual, family, work, and community life. After you have assembled your list, prioritize it. Our Learned Ignorance and Helplessness can hold us back on our jobs and in our relationships. What do you need to know right now? What do you need to start doing yourself, right now? What do you need to learn and act upon right now?

2. Make a list of at least one thing you will learn or start doing in the next seven days. Do something this week for yourself that you usually put off on others because you felt you were helpless. Take a course to enhance your career, or a parenting workshop to enhance your parenting skills, or seek out a counselor for yourself or family members. There are other things you may need to learn, such as cutting the grass and the hedges, how to say no or how to speak up, write a report, be still and know God, or how to pray or fast.

3. Write in your journal. Are you aware of areas of learned helplessness and ignorance in your life?

Church Ministry Application

What outreach ministries or programs do your church have in place to support members who practice learned ignorance or helplessness?
How is God's plan for abundant living being shared with your church ministry?
How effective is your church's evangelism ministry in reaching the spiritually helpless of your community?

A WOMAN DISCOVERS A NEW WAY OF THINKING

For sessions of 90 minutes or more, use the lesson format for PART ONE and PART TWO.

PART ONE

Opening Prayer - 5 minutes
Scripture - 15 minutes
Chapter Highlights* - 10 minutes

PART TWO

Well Lessons
Small Group - 20 minutes
Large Group - 20 minutes
Life Application* - 15 minutes
Closing Prayer - 5 minutes
*Chapter Highlights and Life Application
  Sections are eliminated in 60-minute
  Sessions

For sessions of less than 90 minutes, the Life Application questions may be assigned as homework.

The Samaritan woman is drawn into a dialogue with the Divine by a simple question, 'Will you give me a drink?' ...Had the thought ever crossed the mind of the Samaritan woman, that she could be more than she was at that moment? There was more to life than she was living? She could be greater than her community's opinion and more than her low self-esteem allowed?... The Samaritan woman (is) transformed at the well by a new level of thinking instigated by Jesus, the Christ.
— *Vashti McKenzie*

Lesson Aim

At the end of this two-part Bible Study session, participants should be able to: a) understand the importance of going deeper in their relationship with Jesus; b) consider the advantages of experiencing Jesus beyond the physical level; and c) learn to seek daily the spiritual level of experiencing Jesus through study of the Word of

God and through worship.

"Sir, give me this water so that I won't get thirsty and have to keep coming here to draw water" (John 4:15, NIV).

OPENING PRAYER – 5 Minutes

Open the session with prayer, including the request that God would bless each participant to:

- Seek to go deeper in their relationship with Jesus
- Seek another level of thinking and a renewal of the mind
- Understand that only an experience with Jesus can take you deeper - from a physical to spiritual level of thinking.
- Ask God to capture every thought and bring it into obedience to Christ

Preparation: Prepare two sheets of paper. On one sheet write or type the words "Physical Level of Thinking" and the "#1" on the back of this sheet. On the other sheet write, "Spiritual Level of Thinking," and the "#2" on the back.

SCRIPTURE SEARCH – 15 Minutes

The Scripture reading and Scripture Search sections for this Bible study are combined in an orchestrated dialogue with the class.

Ask for two volunteers and give each one of the prepared white sheets of paper. Explain that when the Scripture verses are read, each will hold up his/her paper when the verse applies to the level of thinking described.

Inform the class that you will be conducting an orchestrated dialogue or role-play. Explain that you will ask students to read a verse and after each reading, one of the volunteers will hold up his/her sheet of paper indicating what level of thinking is described in the verse.

Encourage the class to listen carefully and reflect on the differences between the physical versus spiritual levels of thinking. Ask volunteers to read the following verses:

John 4:11 - "Sir," the woman said, "you have nothing to draw with and the well is deep. Where can you get this living water?"
(The volunteer should hold up sheet #1 for physical thinking)

John 4:12 - "Are you greater than our father Jacob, who gave us the well and drank from it himself, as did also his sons and his flocks and herds?"
(Sheet #1 — physical)

John 4:13-14 - Jesus answered, "Everyone who drinks this water will be thirsty again, but whoever drinks the water I give him will never thirst. Indeed, the water I give him will become in him a spring of water welling up to eternal life." (Sheet #2 — spiritual)

John 4:15 - The woman said to him, "Sir, give me this water so that I won't get thirsty and have to keep coming here to draw water." (Sheet #2 — spiritual)

Point out that the Samaritan woman was drawn into a dialogue with Jesus by a simple question, "Will you give me a drink?" Ask someone to read the account of Nicodemus and Jesus in John 3:1-7 aloud to the group. Discuss the following:

Nicodemus' physical level of thinking about being born again (vv. 3-4)

Jesus' spiritual response (vv. 5-7)

The similarities between Nicodemus' and the Samaritan woman's level of thinking before Jesus told them differently

What we can learn from these examples?

CHAPTER HIGHLIGHTS –
20 Minutes (recommended for 90-minute sessions only)

Using the content of Chapter 7 as background, give a general overview of the chapter. Be sure to include the following topics:

1. A physical vs. spiritual level of thinking
2. Spiritual thinking emerges not from the flesh or the physical, but is born of Christ or the Spirit of God
3. Thinking with the Mind of Christ
4. Physical thinking is a conduit to the spiritual

PART TWO

BIBLE STUDY APPLICATION
Introduction

The Bible Study Application section contains three Well Lessons that provide an opportunity to examine what the Bible says about how participants can experience "a new level of thinking." The discussion of the Well Lessons should confirm that the students understand the basic principles for living at a deeper level of thinking, resulting in a deeper spiritual life. Allow as much time as necessary to encourage free participation and exchange of ideas and insights.

Procedure

Select Small Group Leaders. Ask for volunteers or select three small group leaders and assign each leader a number from 1-3. Ask the small group leaders to write their number on large sheets of white paper so that they can be seen from a distance. (This can also be done beforehand to save time)

Divide into Small Groups. Inform the participants that they will be separated into small groups. Each group will reflect on a different Well Lesson and then present their reflections to the larger group at the end of the study period. The Well Lessons should be assigned as follows:

Group 1: What goes into the mind comes out in our lives (Well Lesson #1)

Group 2: Just because you cannot see it or explain it does not mean it is not real. (Well Lesson #2)

Group 3: Physical solutions are inadequate to solve spiritual problems (Well Lesson #3)

Allow Participants to Count Off by Threes. Then ask them to follow the small group leader who is holding their assigned number. Identify the location of each group. (These locations can also be pre-printed on a sheet of paper, photocopied, and distributed to save time.) Participants should then gather into smaller groups in the designated meeting areas.

Note: If the Bible Study is large, divide into more groups and reassign alternately the same three Well Lessons to each of the additional groups. In this case, possibly more than one group will be reflecting on each of the Well Lessons. If the Bible Study is small, divide into two or three groups and permit each group to discuss as many of the reflections as each group desires. You may also want to include one of the Well Lessons as part of the homework assignment.

Small Group Study

Small Group Leaders

Each group will have one Well Lesson to explore. For each Well Lesson, there are questions and/or related Scripture references to stimulate discussion.

Sharing Insights

After 15 minutes, designate someone to summarize the small group discussion within the large group presentation that follows. The designated person will have five minutes to present.

Large Group Presentations

Reconvene the Group. Call the small groups together.

Explain the Procedure. A representative from each of the small groups will share that group's reflections on the Well Lesson assigned. The large group will be given an opportunity to comment on reflections after all presentations have been made. Remind participants of the large group to be attentive and jot down notes or significant points on which comments may be made at the designated time.

Remind Small Group Representatives of the Time. Each group representative should summarize the group's reflection in less than five minutes. Allow up to five minutes to discuss each group's presentation.

Note: If there were more than four groups, allow each group three minutes to summarize reflections and encourage small group presenters to keep their reflections within the three minutes.

LIFE APPLICATION DISCUSSION*

If time permits, the larger group can then discuss reflections on the Well Words, Well Language, and Well Works sections of their workbook.

Introduction

The Life Application section consists of reflections on the Well Words, Well Language, and Well Works assigned in the Student Book. Participants are asked to share which words personally framed their journey and what steps they will personally take to demonstrate the lessons learned. Discussion should also address the implications for the church as a whole.

Sharing Insights

This discussion should be open-ended and voluntary. The sharing of personal insights or recommendations for church ministry should be encouraged but not required. The group may have much to share. Be mindful of the time and dedicate only 15 minutes to this exercise.

*Answers are not provided for this section of the study because of the personal or specific nature of the reflections.

Preparation For Next Meeting

Assignment. Participants are asked to read Chapter 8, "A Woman Faces Her Past." Review the Well Lessons in preparation for the next session. Encourage them to come to the next session prepared to share their insights on the contents of the next chapter.

CLOSING PRAYER

Form a prayer circle, ask for specific prayer requests and ask several volunteers to pray, keeping the prayer requests in mind.

ANSWERS TO BIBLE STUDY APPLICATION

WELL LESSON #1
What goes into the mind comes out in our lives.

1. Find each verse and describe the nature of the Holy Spirit in guiding our spiritual level of thinking.

John 14:17
The Spirit of truth, the world cannot see nor accept, but he lives with you and will be in you.

John 14:26
The Holy Spirit will teach you all things and will remind you of all things that Jesus has said to you.

1 Corinthians 2:6-9, 14
God provides a secret wisdom that no ruler of the world can understand; only the man with the Spirit can understand the things that come from the Spirit of God.

John 16:13
The Holy Spirit will guide you into all truth.

2. Fill in the columns, according to the Scripture references given, to compare our thoughts to God's thoughts:

Our Thoughts	God's Thoughts
Are not God's Thoughts	**Are not man's thoughts**
Isaiah 55:8	Isaiah 55:8
Are futile, but a breath	**Are profound, deep**
Psalm 94:11	Psalm 92:5

Are filled with every kind of wickedness, evil, greed and depravity Romans 1:29-31	Are true, noble, right, pure, lovely, admirable, excellent, or praiseworthy Philippians 4:8

3. Therefore, what should we do with our thoughts? Write 2 Corinthians 10:5. In this verse, Paul encourages us to surrender our thoughts to obey Christ in all things.

"We demolish arguments and every pretension that sets itself up against the knowledge of God, and we take captive every thought to make it obedient to Christ."

WELL LESSON #2
Just because you cannot see it or explain it does not mean it is not real.

It begins with water. The genius of Jesus is that He used a question to draw the woman into a dialogue that instigated personal involvement... the physical is the conduit to the spiritual. Jesus leads her (the Samaritan woman) from the physical understanding of water to the spiritual understanding of living water as eternal life. — Vashti McKenzie

In many places within the New Testament, Jesus used the "familiar" and the "physical" elements to which the audience could relate and drew them to a deeper understanding of His spiritual teaching. Many times this teaching was conveyed through parables. These parables were indeed stories.

1. Look up each parable. Identify the "familiar" and give the spiritual meaning that Christ conveys for each familiar object:

Luke 8:4-15
The familiar is the seed that the farmer scatters on varied surfaces. Jesus says the seed represents the Word of God, which depending on the response of the hearer, will either be heeded or will not take root.

Luke 15:5-7
The familiar is the lost sheep whose shepherd searches until he finds it. Jesus says the meaning of the lost sheep is that it represents any

sinner who is lost to sin. Followers of Christ must do all that is possible to find the lost sinner. That sinner's repentance is of greatest importance.

Matthew 13:47-50
The familiar is the fishing net that was let down into the lake and caught all kinds of fish. The fishermen separated the good from the bad; kept the good and threw the bad away.

Jesus says the kingdom of heaven is like this net, and at the end of the age, the angels will separate the good from the bad. The good will be spared and the bad will be thrown into the fiery furnace.

2. Jesus leads the Samaritan woman from the physical understanding of water to the spiritual understanding of living water as eternal life. It is so important to note that Jesus leads the Samaritan woman towards transformation and does not leave her to make this spiritual journey by herself.

Like that Samaritan woman, we too, need to rely on Jesus to lead us toward transformation. From the beginning of time, God had prepared for Jesus to lead the way.

The prophets proclaimed it, write:
Isaiah 11:6, NIV
"The wolf will live with the lamb, the leopard will lie down with the goat, the calf and the lion and the yearling together; and a little child will lead them."

John the Baptist declared it, write:
Matthew 3:11, NIV
"I baptize you with water for repentance. But after me will come one who is more powerful than I, whose sandals I am not fit to carry."

Jesus declares the benefits we gain in letting Him lead the way. Write the benefit that each verse presents.

John 10:27 - **Jesus will know us.**
John 12:26 - **Jesus' Father will honor those who follow Him**
Luke 18:29-30 - **Eternal Life**

WELL LESSON #3
Physical solutions are inadequate to solve spiritual problems.

When you encounter the Divine, the stage is set for a transfer. You can obtain a transfer when you give your life to Jesus Christ. Intervention happens in prayer, the study of the Word of God and worship. This transfer gives you access to the spiritual. You begin to see with spiritual eyes. — Vashti McKenzie

What does it mean to see life with spiritual eyes? It means to see life beyond what the senses can reveal; beyond what can be seen with the physical eye, heard with the physical ear, felt with the physical touch, understood with the carnal mind. Jesus shares with His disciples that they have been blessed to see beyond their physical abilities, to observe the spiritual at work.

1. Look up Matthew 13:16-17 and reflect on Jesus' words to His disciples. **Jesus said that their eyes are blessed to see and their ears are blessed to hear. Jesus also said that many prophets and righteous men had longed to see what they had seen, and to hear what they had heard, but these prophets and righteous men did not get the opportunity.**

What had they been blessed to see and hear?
1. To walk with Jesus
2. To see Jesus perform miracles
3. To sit under Jesus' teachings as He spoke parables and instructed them on the kingdom of God

Do you feel that you have received the blessing to see and hear beyond the physical? List some ways in which the blessing of being able to see with spiritual eyes and hear with spiritual ears, have benefited your life. *(Answers will vary)*

2. How are spiritual vision and hearing received? Match the verses with the way the Scriptures say that we receive spiritual vision and hearing.

a. 2 Kings 6:17	**Prayer**
b. Job 42:5	**Afflictions**
c. Matthew 5:8	**Pure heart**
d. John 14:19	**Faith and belief in Jesus Christ**
e. Luke 8:15	**Retain the Word of God in your heart**
f. John 14:17	**The Spirit of Truth dwells in you**

g. Luke 10:38   **Receive Jesus into your home**
h. Luke 10:39   **Sit at Jesus' feet**

3. Read John 7:38, 39a. To whom does the Lord give His Spirit?
"Whoever believes in me, as the Scripture has said, streams of living water will flow from within him." By this God means the Spirit, whom those who believed in Him were later to receive. The Spirit is given to those who believe in Jesus Christ.

4. Look up the following verses that instruct us on the nature of the Spirit.

2 Corinthians 3:6
"The Spirit gives life"

John 4:24
"God is spirit and his worshipers must worship in spirit and in truth"

LIFE APPLICATION
Personal Application
1. Reflect on the times when you have dwelled on a "physical" understanding of things in your life. What were the advantages of such thinking? What were the disadvantages? How did it affect your behaviors?
2. What does the Samaritan woman's experience with Jesus teach you about what you must do to move to another level of thinking in your life?

WELL WORDS
The following Well Words are offered as encouragement when you feel that you are having difficulty moving beyond your current level of thinking to a deeper spiritual level.

Select one Well Word per day or per week. Memorize this Well Word. It is your personal spiritual landmark to help you in your journey.

"...If there is a natural body, there is also a spiritual body" (1 Corinthians 15:44, NIV).

"The spiritual did not come first, but the natural, and after that the spiritual" (1 Corinthians 15:46, NIV).

"So we fix our eyes not on what is seen, but on what is unseen. For what is seen is temporary, but what is unseen is eternal" (2 Corinthians 4:18, NIV).

"Since we live by the Spirit, let us keep in step with the Spirit." (Galatians 5:25, NIV).

"Now the Lord is the Spirit, and where the Spirit of the Lord is, there is freedom" (2 Corinthians 3:17, NIV).

"Do not conform any longer to the pattern of this world, but be transformed by the renewing of your mind" (Romans 12:2, NIV).

"...We take captive every thought to make it obedient to Christ" (2 Corinthians 10:5, NIV).

"...Whatever is true, whatever is noble, whatever is right, whatever is pure, whatever is lovely, whatever is admirable - if anything is excellent and praiseworthy - think about such things" (Philippians 4:8, NIV).

WELL SABBATICAL

As you continue taking your daily planned rest periods, fill your mind with the Word of God. Reflect on the things Paul suggests in Philippians 4:8, and bring every thought under the control of Christ (2 Corinthians 10:5).

Read Romans 8:1-11. Pray that the Holy Spirit will be your teacher and guide to understanding God's Word. Pray and ask God to help you become more spiritual in your thinking, seeing, and understanding (1 Corinthians 2:16). The mind is often so consumed with the physical that it only perceives the world through the five senses.

Be still and know God. Be aware of His presence and allow the Lord to guide you from physical meanderings to spiritual assurance. Daniel prayed for understanding. His answer was delayed for 21 days. It was not a physical obstruction, but a disruption in the spiritual realm (Daniel 10:12-14). As the disciple Stephen was being stoned by a hostile mob, he looked from his earthly physical crises into the spiritual. He saw Jesus standing in heaven at the right hand of the Father (Acts 7).

WELL LANGUAGE

Let the following affirmations of encouragement also guide you in your journey. Write your favorite on a 3x5 or 5x7 file card in a felt-tip pen in your favorite color.

1. A Different Harvest Requires A Different Seed
2. Think Of New Ways To Achieve New Results
3. Think On What Is True, Pure, Lovely, Excellent, Holy, Right, Noble And Praiseworthy
4. I Shall Be Transformed By The Renewing Of My Mind
5. Thoughts Precede Action
6. Godly Thinking Produces Godly Action
7. Let's Get Spiritual

WELL WORKS

1. Spend time reading through the Gospels to discover the questions Jesus asked during his three-year earthly ministry. Here is a sampling of questions to get you started:

- "Do you believe I am able to do this?" Mathew 9:28
- "To what can I compare this generation?" Matthew 11:16
- "And why do you break the command of God for the sake of your tradition?" Matthew 15:3
- "Who do the people say the Son of Man is?" Matthew 16:13
- "What do you want me to do for you?" Luke 18:41
- "Do you believe in the Son of Man?" John 9:35
- "What is the Kingdom of God like? What shall I compare it to?" Luke 13:13

2. Read the questions and let them inspire you to a new level of thinking as you study the Gospels. Begin to discover new realities as you are prompted to become a participant in the spiritual. Remember to ask the Holy Spirit to be your teacher and guide through God's Word.

3. Write in your journal the answer to: Can you be more than you are now?

Church Ministry Application

- Reflect on ways in which churches demonstrate a physical level of thinking? List some examples of physical thinking in the local church.
- What are the affects of this type of thinking upon the church? The community?
- Just as Jesus called the Samaritan woman to a higher level of thinking, God calls the church to higher thinking, which is spiritual. Think about the challenges that prevent churches from reaching spiritual levels of thinking.
- Reflect on how your church is meeting this challenge.

A WOMAN FACES HER PAST

For sessions of 90 minutes or more, use the lesson format for PART ONE and PART TWO.

PART ONE

Opening Prayer - 5 minutes

Scripture Search - 15 minutes

Chapter Highlights* - 15 minutes

PART TWO

Well Lessons

Small Group - 15 minutes

Large Group - 20 minutes

Life Application* - 15 minutes

Closing Prayer - 5 minutes

*Chapter Highlights and Life Application Sections are eliminated in 60-minute Sessions

For sessions of less than 90 minutes, the Life Application questions may be assigned as homework.

If you want to talk about long — time problems, talk to the Samaritan woman. She had a persistent problem. She was a woman with a past.... It was as if Jesus responded, "Go home and get your past. It is the long-time problem that needs to be dealt with first. We'll talk about Living Water after you have retrieved your husband." — *Vashti McKenzie*

Lesson Aim

At the end of this Bible study session, the participants should be able to: a) realize that they must not hide behind their past; b) begin a process to examine their past that includes personal reflection: retrieval and retrospect; c) invite the presence of Christ into this process of reflection; and d) pray for courage, strength and healing as he or she faces the past.

"Go, call your husband, and come back" (John 4:16, NIV).

PART ONE

OPENING PRAYER – 5 Minutes

Open the session with a prayer of thanksgiving for the Disciplines of the Well and the varied Well Sabbaticals that the participants will experience in this study. Pray that God will bless each participant to:

- Understand the importance of dealing with past experiences
- Recognize that they cannot move on to new levels of thinking and spiritual growth until they have dealt with things of the past that might be standing in the way
- Accept the presence of Jesus in their journey as they reflect on past experiences
- Celebrate the divine intervention of the Holy Spirit to guide them beyond the unresolved issues of the past to resolution today.

SCRIPTURE SEARCH – 15 Minutes

Ask someone to read John 4:15-18 aloud and others to answer the following questions:

1. Jesus tells the woman that the water He shall give will make a person never to thirst again. (v. 14) What response does the woman give Jesus?
She asked Jesus for this water so that she wouldn't thirst anymore, nor have need to return to Jacob's well to draw water. (v. 15)

2. Did the woman realize what Jesus was talking about? Explain your answer.
No. She thought that Jesus meant physical water rather than spiritual fulfillment.

3. What was Jesus' response to her?
Go, call your husband and come here. (v. 16)

4. What did the woman say?
I have no husband. (v. 17)

5. How did Jesus then respond?
You have well said, "I have no husband," for you have had five husbands, and the one whom you now have is not your husband (vv. 17-18).

6. Discuss why Jesus asked the woman to call her husband. Include the following points:

a. Jesus wanted to help the woman deal with her past: five husbands, a lack of acceptance within the community, broken relationships, etc.

b. Jesus wanted to deal with her spiritual condition.

c. Jesus wanted to acquaint her with His divine presence, which would bring her healing and restoration.

7. Reflect on how Jesus' question about her husband opened the door of her past that she might have been trying to hide. What reality did she now have to face? **Answers will vary.**

CHAPTER HIGHLIGHTS –
15 Minutes (recommended for 90-minute sessions only)

Using the content of Chapter 8 as background, give a general overview of the chapter. Be sure to include the following topics:

1. We cannot hide behind our past
2. Nothing changes without personal transformation
3. Personal transformation begins with personal reflection and consists of two components: retrieval and retrospect
4. Retrieval and retrospect must be done in the presence of Christ to experience healing and restoration.

PART TWO

BIBLE STUDY APPLICATION
Introduction

The Bible Study Application section contains four Well Lessons that provide an opportunity to examine what the Bible says about overcoming debilitating problems and patterns.

Allow as much time as necessary to encourage free participation and exchange of ideas and insights.

Procedure

Select Small Group Leaders. Ask for volunteers or select four small group leaders, assign each leader a number from 1-4 and ask them to write their number on large sheets of paper so that they can be seen from a distance. (This can also be done beforehand to save time).

Divide into Small Groups. Inform the participants that they will be separated into small groups. Each group will reflect on a different Well Lesson and then present their reflections to the larger group at the end of the study period. The Well Lessons should be assigned as follows:

Group 1: Confront the past if you want to be a resolved person. (Well Lesson #1)

Group 2: Jesus gives unconditional belonging, acceptance and love (Well Lesson #2)

Group 3: As long as we remain unresolved, history will keep repeating itself. (Well Lesson #3)

Group 4: Forgiveness is available every day.

Allow Participants to Count Off By Fours. Then ask them to follow the small group leader who is holding their assigned number. Identify the location of each group. (These locations can also be pre-printed on a sheet of paper, photocopied, and distributed to save time). Participants should then gather into smaller groups in the designated meeting areas.

Note: If the Bible Study is large, divide into more groups and reassign alternately the same four Well Lessons to each of the additional groups. In this case, possibly more than one group will be reflecting on each of the Well Lessons. If the Bible Study is small, divide into two groups and permit each group to discuss as many of the reflections as each group desires. You may also want to include some of the Well Lessons as part of the homework assignment.

Small Group Study
Small Group Leaders

Each group will have one Well Lesson to explore. For each Well Lesson, there are questions and/or related Scripture references to stimulate discussion.

Sharing Insights

After 15 minutes, designate someone to summarize the small group discussion within the large group presentation that follows. The designated person will have five minutes to present.

Large Group Presentations
Reconvene the Group. Call the small groups together.

Explain the Procedure. A representative from each of the small groups will share that group's reflections on the Well Lesson assigned. The large group will be given an opportunity to comment on reflections after all presentations have been made. Remind participants of the large group to be attentive and jot down notes or significant points on which comments may be made at the designated time.

Remind Small Group Representatives of the Time. Each group representative should summarize the group's reflection in less than five minutes. Allow up to five minutes to discuss each group's presentation.

Note: If there were more than four groups, allow each group three minutes to summarize reflections and encourage small group presenters to keep their reflections within the three minutes.

LIFE APPLICATION DISCUSSION*

If time permits, the larger group can then discuss reflections on the Well Words, Well Language and Well Works sections of their workbook.

Introduction

The Life Application section consists of reflections on the Well Words, Well Language and Well Works assigned in the Student Book. Participants are asked to share which words personally framed their journey and what steps they will personally take to demonstrate the lessons learned. Discussion should also address the implications for the church as a whole.

Sharing Insights

This discussion should be open-ended and voluntary. The sharing of personal insights or recommendations for church ministry should be encouraged but not required. The group may have much to share. Be mindful of the time and dedicate only 15 minutes to this exercise.

*Answers are not provided for this section of the study because of the personal or specific nature of the reflections.

Preparation For Next Meeting

Assignment. Participants are asked to read Chapter 9, "A Woman Without Excuses." Review the Well Lessons in preparation for the next session. Encourage them to come to the next session prepared to share their insights on the contents of the next chapter.

CLOSING PRAYER

Form a prayer circle and ask for specific prayer requests. Then ask several volunteers to pray, keeping the prayer requests in mind.

ANSWERS TO BIBLE STUDY APPLICATION

WELL LESSON #1
Confront the past if you want to be a resolved person.

It was as if Jesus responded "Go home and get your past. It is the long-time problem that needs to be dealt with first." We'll talk about Living Water after you have retrieved your husband...The woman could not get the Living Water like she was. There had to be an adjustment. Remember nothing changes without personal transformation. But only after facing her past. — Vashti McKenzie

"Go, call your husband, and come back." John 4:16 (NIV)
Each of us has had experiences that we would choose to forget: past disappointments, sins, and mistakes. This lesson stresses the fact that we cannot hide from our pasts. In order to experience restoration and transformation, we must confront our past experiences.

The following people had to deal with their pasts, and each experienced transformation as a result of doing so. Match the person with the personal transformation that occurred in his or her life.

Bible Personality	Personal Transformation
A Paul (Acts 9:1-22)	From a persecutor of Christians to a proselyte for Christ
B. Mary Magdalene (Luke 8:1-2)	From a woman with 7 demons to a minister of substance
C. Thief on the Cross (Luke 23:40-43)	From a sinner facing damnation to a saved sinner with a promise of being with Jesus in paradise
D. Adulteress woman (John 8:3-11)	From adulterer to a repentant woman free from the sin of adultery

2. What brought about the transformation in their lives?
Each person experienced an encounter with Jesus.
It is important to note that sometimes transformation occurs after a person has gone through difficult times. Personal reflections at this point, although, painful, bring about transformation.

The following Biblical personalities experienced moments of personal transformation while in crisis or difficult times. Look up the Bible passages below and describe the transformations that occurred in each person's life.

Genesis 28:20-22; 32:9-12
Jacob, a refugee driven from his home for stealing his brother's birthright, finds himself in a dream where God unfolds His plan for Jacob and his descendants. Jacob awakens and vows allegiance to the Lord in exchange for promised protection and blessing. Jacob's reflections and transformation are articulated in his prayer, found in 32:9-12.

Luke 15:11-18
The Prodigal son took his inheritance, wasted it and found himself with nothing. Upon personal reflection, "he came to his senses" (v. 17), and decided to return home and repent of his sins. His personal reflection led to transformation, as he returned home and was well received by his father.

Psalm 51:1-3
David prays for forgiveness after his affair with Bathsheba and his murder of her husband Uriah. The personal reflection on his sinful acts led him to repentance and transformation.

WELL LESSON #2
Jesus gives unconditional belonging, acceptance, and love.

When we retrieve and contemplate the past, it is important to invite the presence of Christ, who will provide support to us as we journey. Look up the verses below and write about some of the promises that the Lord will provide to you as you deal with your past.

1 John 1:9
If I confess my sins, God will forgive them. God will purify me from all unrighteousness.

Romans 12:19
Do not revenge, but let the Lord deal with vengeance. The Lord says vengeance is his.

Psalm 27
There is nothing to fear - The Lord is my light and my salvation.

Isaiah 41:10
Do not fear because God is with you. God will strengthen, help and uphold you.

Matthew 28:20
Jesus promises to be with His disciples always.

Romans 8:28
In all things God works for the good of those who love him.

WELL LESSON #3
As long as we remain unresolved, history will keep repeating itself.

Read the accounts of the following Bible personalities. What unresolved issues do you think they had? How may this have kept them from moving forward and receiving transformation?

Michal (Saul's daughter) (1 Samuel 18:20-21; 2 Samuel 3:13-16; 2 Samuel 6:17-23)
Answers may include Saul tried to use Michal as a weapon against David; Saul gave her in marriage to someone else and she was later made to leave him and marry David; her father's insecurities could have been passed along to her.

Cain (Genesis 4:1-12)
Answers may include: Cain was jealous of his younger brother; he didn't want to give God his best, but was upset when his brother did.

Tamar (Genesis 38:1-19)
Answers may include: Tamar may have felt regret and grief for losing her two husbands; she may have felt unworthy because of Onan's treatment ; she may have felt slighted by Judah, who refused to let her marry his third son and made her return to her father's home.

WELL LESSON #4
Forgiveness is available everyday.

It does not matter whether your issues are ancient, recent history or current events, when you confess, God is faithful to forgive (1 John 1:9). This is not a license to do as you please. It is the escape button on your lifestyle computer to end an unproductive program or the means to reboot your life so you can reprogram your system according to the Word and the will of God.
— Vashti McKenzie

Read the following parables. What lessons do they teach about forgiveness?

Parables of the Lost Sheep and the Lost Coin (Luke 15:1-10)
God rejoices when we repent.

Parable of the Unmerciful Servant (Matthew 18:21-35)
God willingly forgives our huge debt and we are expected to willingly forgive others as well.

LIFE APPLICATION
Personal Application
It is in these moments of reflection that we must remember the Word of God, the promises and assurances that it reveals to us about overcoming our past experiences.

WELL WORDS

The following Well Words are offered as encouragement when you feel that you are having difficulty overcoming your past. Select one Well Word per day or per week. Memorize this Well Word. It is your personal spiritual landmark to help you in your journey.

1. "Shake off your dust, rise up, sit enthroned, O Jerusalem. Free yourself from the chains on your neck, O captive Daughter of Zion." (Isaiah 52:2, NIV)
2. "Have mercy on me, O God, according to your unfailing love, according to your compassion blot out my transgressions" (Psalm 51:1, NIV).
3. "Therefore do not worry about tomorrow, for tomorrow will worry about itself. Each day has enough trouble of its own" (Matthew 6:34, NIV).
4. "Since we have these promises, dear friends, let us purify ourselves from everything that contaminates body and spirit, perfecting holiness out of reverence for God." (2 Corinthians 7:1, NIV).
5. "Therefore, if anyone is in Christ, he is a new creation; the old has gone, the new has come!" (2 Corinthians 5:17, NIV)
6. "Brothers, I do not consider myself yet to have taken hold of it. But one thing I do: Forgetting what is behind and straining toward what is ahead." (Philippians 3:13, NIV).

WELL SABBATICAL

- A planned rest period is an excellent place to begin reflection in the presence of Christ. Take as long as necessary to disturb the dust of denial, scratching beneath the surface of living to survey past thoughts, decisions, and actions.
- Search to see if there are any recycled behaviors and habits that inhibit or debilitate. Examine the behaviors and habits that have kept you in your personal wilderness and can strengthen you in the Promised Land of resolution.
- Retrieve the past. Remember, going back is not to get back or to stay back, it is to clear the air of the dust that clouds our vision and clogs our mission. Reflect upon it through the eyes of Christ and in the Word of God. A good promise book that lists God's promises may help you see yesterday in the light of the Gospel. When you disturb the dust of sin, read Psalm 51 or 1 John 1:5-10; a trial, Psalm 26; vengeance, Romans 12:17-21; depression, Psalm 16, Isaiah 61:1-4; illness, Psalm 23, Mark 1:29-34; James 5:14-16; disasters, Romans 8:31-19; prejudice, Ephesians 2:11-22 or fear, Psalm 27.

- It's good to take just as much time during your Sabbatical to remember the wonderful and marvelous experiences of yesterday. The past also includes the great, the very good, and the good. Go treasure hunting for the good and take others with you. It is good to up-link with your friends, instead of always downloading. Gather your old high school yearbooks for a "The Way We Were" gathering. Laugh at the old hairstyles and fashions. Make a "good times" scrapbook. Post photos of fond memories on your mirrors, and refrigerator doors. Keep the good ever before you. It is just as valuable to be acquainted with these high mountaintop experiences. They can keep you afloat in your off seasons. Strengths revisited are like medicine to the spirit. Joys recalled are like a shot in the arm. The remembrance of them helps you to go from strength to strength. Look for the good and celebrate.
- If the confrontation and contemplation processes are still too hard to bear, the prayerful assistance of a pastor or counselor could prove beneficial.

WELL LANGUAGE

Let the following affirmations of encouragement also guide your journey. Write your favorite on a 3x5 or 5x7 file card in a felt-tip pen in a color you prefer.
1. I am ready to Move On!
2. Reflect and Resolve
3. Confront, Contemplate and Create New Beginnings
4. Look Back and Lean Forward
5. Look for the Good and Celebrate

WELL WORKS

The following Well Works are provided to help you take steps to demonstrate your new commitment to live out the lessons learned in this session.
1. If you're in a group, sit in a circle. Place an empty bowl in the center of circle, either on the floor or on a table.
2. Each participant should hold a glass of water, representing the tears of the past, all the tears you have cried without resolution. The water also represents the tears of the present because of the influence of the past.

3. In the presence of Christ and in view of God's Word, each woman now prayerfully and carefully considers personal reflection, engaging in the acts of confrontation and contemplation of past issues. Ask the Divine for intervention of the Holy Spirit to guide women and men into all truth, and move them toward resolution.

4. Stand when ready to move beyond unresolved issues: habits that hurt, the fear that inhibits, addictive reactions, self-inflicted wounds. tragedies, deaths, regrets, rejections, childhood residue of being alone, doing too much or not enough, and sins of others upon your life. Carry the glass to the empty bowl. one at a time. Pour out the tears slowly saying, "I am ready to move on!" Continue to repeat the phrase as all the water is poured into the bowl.

5. Having released your tears, begin to thank God. Praise God for intentionally meeting you at the well of personal reflection. Thank God for the invitation to resolution and personal transformation. "Now to him who is able to do immeasurably more than we ask or imagine, according to his power that is at work within us" (Ephesians 3:20, NIV).

Church Ministry Application

Describe a negative past experience in the life of your church that resulted in unresolved issues.

- What affect have these unresolved issues had on the following?
- The spiritual life of the church?
- The growth of the church?
- The presence of harmony and unity among the membership?
- The vision of the church?

This session has emphasized the importance of dealing with unresolved issues of the past through reflection. What ideas do you have for bringing God's resolution to your church's unresolved past experience(s)?

Pray for the presence of God to enter this process of reflection.

A WOMAN WITHOUT EXCUSES

For sessions of 90 minutes or more, use the lesson format for PART ONE and PART TWO.

PART ONE

Opening Prayer - 5 minutes

Scripture - 15 minutes

Chapter Highlights* - 10 minutes

PART TWO

Well Lessons

Small Group - 20 minutes

Large Group - 20 minutes

Life Application* - 15 minutes

Closing Prayer - 5 minutes

*Chapter Highlights and Life Application Sections are eliminated in 60-minute Sessions

For sessions of less than 90 minutes, the Life Application questions may be assigned as homework.

The Samaritan woman came to the well with lots of excuses. Jesus methodically peeled away her excuses one by one. Jesus was teaching her to live life decisively. Life without excuses is living a decisive life. — Vashti McKenzie

Lesson Aim

At the end of this Bible study session, students will be able to a) realize that painful past experiences can become bridges to success in future challenges, b) know that the difference between success and failure is often dependent upon how you use what you have, c) admit that excuses are often used to get favor, shift blame, or justify our behavior, d) decide to dispense with excuses that hinder potential.

"What you have just said is quite true" (John 4:18, NIV).

PART ONE

OPENING PRAYER – 5 minutes

Open the session with a prayer of thanksgiving for:
- The opportunity to study *"Journey to the Well."*
- The participants who have been on this Journey experience.
- The Disciplines learned and lived during the Journey: The Well Lessons, Well Words, Well Sabbaticals, Well Language and Well Works

SCRIPTURE SEARCH – 15 minutes

Ask someone to read John 4:18 and others to answer the following questions:

1. To what was Jesus referring when He told the Samaritan woman that what she had just said was true? **She had no husband.**

2. What was Jesus' reaction when she made this statement?
It was one of commendation. "You have told the truth."

3. Jesus, knowing the woman's past life, told her to go and call her husband. What might have been His reason for doing this?
It was an attempt to make her acknowledge her plight; to let her know that He was all-knowing; and that He was not just a Jew, but the Messiah.

4. Ask volunteers to read the following passages of Scripture. Discuss each passage to explore what the Bible says about telling the truth.

Psalms 15:2, 5b
Truth is a requirement for anyone who will remain in God's favor/presence.

Psalms 51:6
God desires truth in the inward part.

Ephesians 4:25
Truth is necessary because we are members one of another.

CHAPTER HIGHLIGHTS –
20 Minutes (recommended for 90 minute sessions only.)

Using the content of Chapter 9 as background, give a general overview of the chapter. Be sure to include the following topics.

1. Excuses as crutches
2. Excuses as decisions
3. Living without excuses is living a decisive life.
4. The "Three D" choice method for women Who Do Too Much (include the fourth and fifth Ds)

drop   **deny**
delay   **discern**
delegate

PART TWO

BIBLE STUDY APPLICATION
Introduction

The Bible Study Application section contains three Well Lessons that provide an opportunity to examine what the Bible says about excuses and the need to dispense with those that hinder us from reaching our potential. Allow as much time as necessary to encourage free participation and exchange of ideas and insights.

Procedure

Select Small Group Leaders. Ask for volunteers or select three small group leaders and assign a number to each leader. Ask the small group leaders to write their numbers on large sheets of white paper so that they can be seen from a distance. (This can be done beforehand to save time).

Divide into Small Groups. Inform the participants that they will be separated into two groups. Each group will study a different Well Lesson and then present their reflections to the larger group at the end of the study period.

The Well Lessons should be assigned as follows:

Group 1: Stop making excuses and start making decisions.

Group 2: It's not what we have that matters, it's what we do with it.

Group 3: There are always choices to be made.

Allow Participants to Count Off by Threes. Then ask them to follow the small group leader who is holding their assigned number. Identify the location of each group. (These locations can also be pre-printed on a sheet of paper, photocopied, and distributed to save time.) Participants should then gather into smaller groups in the designated meeting areas.

Note: If the Bible study is large, divide into more groups and reassign alternately the same three Well Lessons to each of the additional groups. In this case, possibly more than one group will be reflecting on each of the Well Lessons. If the Bible Study is small, remain in one group to discuss all three Well Lessons.

Small Group Study
Small Group Leaders
Each group will have one Well Lesson to explore. For each Well Lesson, there are questions and/or related Scripture references to stimulate discussion.

Sharing Insights
After 15 minutes, designate someone to summarize the small group discussion within the large group presentation that follows. The designated person will have five minutes to present.

Large Group Presentations
Reconvene the group. Call the small groups together.

Explain the procedure. A representative from each of the small groups will share that group's reflections on the Well Lesson assigned. The large group will have an opportunity to comment on reflections after all presentations have been made. Remind participants of the large group to be attentive and jot down notes or significant points on which comments may be made at the designated time.

Remind Small Group Representatives of the Time. Each group representative should summarize the group's reflection in less than five minutes. Allow up to five minutes to discuss each group's presentation.

Note: If there were more than three groups, allow each group three minutes to summarize reflections and encourage small group presenters to keep their reflections within the three minutes.

LIFE APPLICATION DISCUSSION*
If time permits, the larger group can then discuss reflections on the Well Words, Well Language and Well Works sections of their workbook.

Introduction
The Life Application section consists of reflections on the Well Words, Well Language and Well Works assigned in the Student Book. Participants are asked to

share which Words personally framed their journey and what steps they will personally take to demonstrate the lessons learned. Discussion should also address the implications for the church as a whole.

Sharing Insights

The discussion should be open-ended and voluntary. The sharing of personal insights or recommendations for church ministry should be encouraged but not required. The group may have much to share. Be mindful of the time and dedicate only 10 minutes to this exercise.

*Answers are not provided for this section of the study because of the personal or specific nature of the reflections.

Preparation For Next Meeting

Assignment. Participants are asked to read Chapter 10, "A Woman Takes An Opportunity." Review the Well Lessons in preparation for the next session. Remind students to take the time to enjoy the Well Sabbatical and to pen any new experiences or revelations. Encourage them to come to the next session prepared to share their insights on the content of the next chapter. You may also want to assign small groups or specific Well Lessons to facilitate next week's meeting time. Encourage the class to do Well Sabbatical while preparing for next session.

CLOSING PRAYER

Invite all to pray individually for the ability to stop making excuses and begin using whatever God has given them to the best of their ability. You may close with a prayer of thanksgiving for the forgiveness of God's people through Jesus Christ.

ANSWERS TO BIBLE STUDY APPLICATION

WELL LESSON #1
Stop making excuses and start making decisions.

"What you have just said is quite true" (John 4:18, NIV).

There are many Bible stories about people who made excuses, but were not "let off the hook" by God. When they made the decision to rise above their excuses, God used them in many ways.

Look up the following verses and describe the success stories of several of these people:

Exodus 4:10-12

God used Moses in many ways — not the least of which was to become the person by whom the Law of God was given. In addition, God used Moses as the liberator/spokesperson for the children of Israel. God told Moses that he would send him to Pharaoh to bring His people out of Egypt. One of the excuses that Moses made was that he did not have eloquent speech. The Lord disregarded Moses' excuse, and asked him who had made his mouth — "Is it not I, the Lord?" God then made Moses a promise..."Go; I will help you speak and will teach you what to say." Moses obeyed, and God used him despite his speech impediment.

Judges 4:9

Deborah lived at a time when it was not common for women to take the lead. When God promised Israel's deliverance to her, she sent for Barak and gave him the message that God had given her. Barak refused to go to battle without Deborah at his side. Deborah, convinced of God's leading, chose to go with him. She made no excuses, instead, decided to not let her gender prevent God's plan from being carried out. She told Barak that he would not receive the honor because the Lord would "hand Sisera" over to a woman.

Acts 22:10, 14

As a new convert, Paul could have made many excuses. He could have talked about his past life persecuting the church. Paul had a less than desirable past, but excuses, God would not allow. He was sent to Damascus to get his basic training and instructions, and then told that he had been chosen to be "God's witness to all men of what he had seen and heard."

WELL LESSON #2
It's not what we have that matters; it's what we do with it.

The fourth farmer was grateful for what he had... He did what he could with what he had...He partnered with God to live beyond his excuses.
— *Vashti McKenzie*

A few years ago, the newspapers carried the story of Osceola McCarty of the state of Mississippi. She amassed a considerable amount of wealth, making her living as a washerwoman. Although she was told there was no money to be made by washing and ironing, this did not deter her. She saved her money by living modestly, refusing to own a car, or many of life's luxuries. Out of her meager earnings, she was able to give thousands of dollars to the University of Southern Mississippi for scholarships.

1. In what way does her story parallel the story of the five barley loaves and the two fish that were used to feed the crowd? (John 6:9-12)
Her little became much.

2. What can be learned from her story relative to the Well Lesson?
She exemplified the Well Lesson: "It's not what we have that matters it's what we do with it." She saved small amounts until it became a large amount.

3. How does Ms. McCarty's story compare to the parable of the talents (Luke 25:14-30)
She multiplied the little she had like the servant with five talents and unlike the servant with one talent.

WELL LESSON #3
There are always choices to be made.

Jesus gave us the power to choose. Like the woman at the well, we can never be successful or experience transformation while victimized by excuses.
— *Vashti McKenzie*

Match the following Scripture references with the person who made the choice:

A. "But if serving the Lord seems undesirable to you, then choose for yourselves this day whom you will serve, whether the gods your forefathers served beyond the River, or the gods of the Amorites, in whose land you are living. But as for me and my household, we will serve the Lord." Joshua 24:15

B. "I will bless the Lord at all times; his praise will be on my lips." Psalm 34:1

C. "Martha, Martha," the Lord answered, "you are worried and upset about many things, but only one thing is needed. Mary has chosen what is better, and it will not be taken away from her." Luke 10:42

D. "He chose to be mistreated along with the people of God rather than to enjoy the pleasures of sin for a short time." Hebrews 11:25

Joshua A
Moses D
Mary C
David B

LIFE APPLICATION
Personal Application
Reflect on the times you have used excuses to evade facing the real reason why you do not do some things that you should do. Place a check mark beside your reason for using the excuse and write your reflections in the space provided.

_____To get special treatment
_____To apologize for your bad behavior
_____To shift blame to someone or something else
_____To justify your behavior

_____
_____
_____

During your reflections, ponder the fact that excuses build walls that lock us in, preventing us from reaching our potential. Decide to dismiss unfounded excuses and do as the ant when he reached a crack in the sidewalk—use another method to get the straw across.

WELL WORDS
The following Well Words will remind you that you are without excuses:

"This day I call heaven and earth as witnesses against you that I have set before you life and death, blessings and curses. Now choose life, so that you and your children may live" (Deuteronomy 30:19, NIV).

"You did not choose me, but I chose you and appointed you to go and bear fruit—fruit that will last. Then the Father will give you whatever you ask in my name" (John 15:16, NIV).

"But God chose the foolish things of the world to shame the wise; God chose the weak things of the world to shame the strong" (1 Corinthians 1:27, NIV).

"But you are a chosen people, a royal priesthood, a holy nation, a people belonging to God, that you may declare the praises of him who called you out of darkness into his wonderful light" (1 Peter 2:9, NIV).

"For the wages of sin is death, but the gift of God is eternal life in Christ Jesus our Lord" (Romans 5:23, NIV).

"Choose my instruction instead of silver, knowledge rather than choice gold" (Proverbs 8:10, NIV).

"Trust in the Lord with all your heart, and lean not on your own understanding; in all your ways acknowledge him, and he will make your paths straight" (Proverbs 3:5-6, NIV).

"Everything is permissible—but not everything is beneficial. Everything is permissible—but not everything is constructive" (1 Corinthians 10:23, NIV).

WELL SABBATICAL
Take your sabbatical outside. Take a walk in the park, a leisurely stroll in a garden, or take a stroll where you can enjoy the sights and sounds of nature. Take the time to enjoy a sunrise or a sunset for a change. Record in your journal what you saw, smelled, or touched. Don't make excuses: make a decision to find the time for this outdoor sabbatical. Fresh air works in an amazing way to clear our thinking. Movement increases the flow of oxygen to the blood. Circulation increases the flow to the brain. A Change of scenery sometimes gives us a new perspective, as we get up-close and personal in our own lives. We need to shut off and push back from the daily in-office, in-home, or inside routines of our lives.

It wouldn't hurt to bring the outdoors indoors. Buy fresh flowers for yourself or purchase a living plant. Light a fire in the fireplace, if you have one. Otherwise, boil fresh cinnamon sticks or a drop of pine oil in hot water on the stove; the aroma is fresh and delicious. Open the doors and windows where you live or work to let fresh air in for a while.

Be still, breathe deeply, and listen for the still, small voice of God. Breathe, listen, and write what the Spirit tells you to write in your journal.

WELL LANGUAGE
1. Your are capable.
2. It is within your reach.
3. The Lord will be your helper.
4. Nothing beats a try.
5. I make decision and not excuses.
6. I am a chooser, not a beggar.

WELL WORKS
1. Face up to one of your excuses. We have lived with our excuses for too long. We have taken them everywhere, packed carefully in our backpacks and briefcases, hauling them from one event to the next. Facing the truth of our excuses can be a painful process, but in the presence of Christ, we can identify them. Jesus is a patient Deity who will methodically peel the layers of excuses away until we receive our power to choose.

That is not to say there are never any good reasons why our forward progress is impeded. It only means that we can choose how to respond to it — as an obstacle, or as stepping-stones.

2. Brainstorm at least one way to respond to an existing challenge in your life. Write in your journal what you can do until the situation changes. When you have completed one idea, move to the next. For example: Are you unemployed with time on your hands? You can sit and sulk at home or volunteer your time and talents at church or a non-profit organization. Does debt or bad credit burden you? Seek professional credit counseling before seeking a loan or more credit cards. This service is free in some areas. Cut up your credit cards and cut down your budget. Make the decision to do those things that lead to debt-free living.

3. Write in your journal a list of things you can do until change comes.

Church Ministry Application
Find out from church ministry leaders if help is needed in their respective departments.

Put a Want-Ad page in your church newsletter or on the church bulletin board. List areas of church ministries (Sunday School, Vacation Bible School, evangelism, etc.) where help is needed.

Eliminate the possibility of excuses by indicating that for those who lack adequate experience, training will be offered.

A WOMAN TAKES AN OPPORTUNITYY

For sessions of 90 minutes or more, use the lesson format for PART ONE and PART TWO.

PART ONE

Opening Prayer - 5 minutes

Scripture - 15 minutes

Chapter Highlights* - 15 minutes

PART TWO

Well Lessons

Small Group - 15 minutes

Large group - 20 minutes

Life Application* - 15 minutes

Closing Prayer - 5 minutes

*Chapter Highlights and Life Application Sections are eliminated in 60-minute Sessions

For sessions of less than 90 minutes, the Life Application questions may be assigned as homework.

This woman was faced with an opportunity created by what Howard Thurman would call a "Teachable Moment." A Teachable Moment is a crack in our armor through which God can penetrate our lives. Such things as crises, disappointments, pain and even sudden, unexpected encounters with God create these moments. — Vashti McKenzie

Lesson Aim

At the end of this Bible study session, the participants should be able to: a) reflect on the *Teachable Moments* that have occurred in their lives; b) identify and pray for God's strength to overcome the learning disabilities that threaten to disrupt opportunities; c) realize that many times opportunities come when we least expect them; d) realize that God often breaks into our lives on the heels of crisis and difficult times; and e) accept that God recognizes your worth.

"'Sir,' the woman said, 'I can see that you are a prophet. Our fathers worshiped on this mountain, but you Jews claim that the place where we must worship is in Jerusalem.' Jesus declared. 'Believe me, woman, a time is coming when you will worship the Father neither on this mountain nor in Jerusalem'" (John 4:19-21, NIV).

PART ONE

OPENING PRAYER – 5 Minutes

Open the session with a prayer of thanksgiving for the Disciplines of the Well and the varied Well Sabbaticals that the participants will experience in this study. Pray that God will bless each participant to:

- Learn to recognize and take advantage of the Teachable Moments with which God wants to bless them
- Be prepared for the many opportunities that will come when they least expect them
- Consider the times that Jesus blessed them with unexpected opportunities and how they benefited from those experiences
- Ask forgiveness for the many missed, messed up or ignored opportunities from which you failed to learn; and pray for strength to move on!
- Make a commitment with God to seize, nurture, and make the most of all opportunities.

SCRIPTURE SEARCH – 15 Minutes

Ask someone to read John 4:19-21 aloud to the group. Use the following statements and questions to review the facts from this Scripture passage:

1. The woman calls Jesus a prophet. Why?
Because Jesus had just told her all about her life - her past five husbands and the man with whom she now lived who was not her husband

2. The woman then seems to change the subject and begins talking to Jesus about what?
She talks to Jesus about the place or the location where one ought to worship.

3. Describe the tone of her conversation.

She seems to be trying to enter a debate: Our Fathers (the Samaritans) worship on this mountain...but you Jews say that Jerusalem is the place where worship is to occur.

4. How did Jesus respond?

Jesus says that there is coming a time when neither location - this mountain or Jerusalem would be required for the worship of God. Those places would become obsolete.

5. Why did the woman address the subject of the place of worship?
Suggestions might include the following:

She wanted to skip the subject. Jesus had just asked her to call her husband and by doing so, forced her to deal with her past, her sins, and her possible shame. She didn't want to talk any more about those men in her life, that past, nor the sinful present.

She recognized Jesus as a prophet and wanted him to know that she, too, was a religious person.

She acknowledges now her sins and seeks to find a place to worship, to offer sacrifices and to ask forgiveness.

She recognizes the divine in Jesus and trusts that He will reveal to her the truth and lead her to a place of worship where she can deal with her sinfulness.

6. In this passage, the woman seizes the opportunity given to her by Jesus. What was the opportunity she seized?

She engaged in a conversation with Jesus, which brought about personal revelation and the removal of barriers between her and God.

CHAPTER HIGHLIGHTS –
15 Minutes (recommended for 90-minute sessions only)

Using the content of Chapter 10 as background, give a general overview of the chapter. Be sure to include the following topics:

- The importance of the Teachable Moments in our lives

- God intentionally meets us in our Teachable Moments and provides opportunities for change
- Teachable Moments are often interrupted by learning disabilities
- Many times opportunities come when we least expect them
- Learn to be vigilant; take advantage of all opportunities with which God wants to bless you.

PART TWO

BIBLE STUDY APPLICATION

Introduction

The Bible Study Application section contains three Well Lessons that provide an opportunity to examine what the Bible says about how to live through our past experiences. Allow as much time as necessary to encourage free participation and exchange of ideas and insights.

Procedure

Select Small Group Leaders. Ask for volunteers or select three small group leaders and assign each leader a number from 1-3. Ask the small group leaders to write their number on large sheets of paper so that they can be seen from a distance. (This can also be done beforehand to save time).

Divide into Small Groups. Inform the participants that they will be separated into small groups. Each group will reflect on a different Well Lesson and then present their reflections to the larger group at the end of the study period. The Well Lessons should be assigned as follows:

Group 1: Learn to take advantage of and nurture opportunities. (Well Lesson #1)

Group 2: The Living Water Jesus provides brings you beyond the left over crumbs society has to offer. (Well Lesson #2)

Group 3: Teachable Moments: Opportunities can be teachable moments and teachable moments can be opportunities. (Well Lesson #3)

Allow Participants to Count Off By Threes. Then ask them to follow the small group leader who is holding their assigned number. Identify the location of each group. (These locations can also be pre-printed on a sheet of paper, photocopied, and distributed to save time). Participants should then gather into smaller groups in the designated meeting areas.

Note: If the Bible Study is large, divide into more groups and reassign alternately the same three Well Lessons to each of the additional groups. In this case, possibly more than one group will be reflecting on each of the Well Lessons. If the Bible Study is small, divide into two groups and permit each group to discuss as many of the reflections as each group desires. You may also want to include Well Lesson 3 as part of the homework assignment.

Small Group Study
Small Group Leaders
Each group will have one Well Lesson to explore. For each Well Lesson, there are questions and/or related Scripture references to stimulate discussion.
Sharing Insights
After 15 minutes, designate someone to summarize the small group discussion within the large group presentation that follows. The designated person will have five minutes to present.

Large Group Presentations
Reconvene the Group. Call the small groups together.

Explain the Procedure. A representative from each of the small groups will share that group's reflections on the Well Lesson assigned. The large group will be given an opportunity to comment on reflections after all presentations have been made. Remind participants of the large group to be attentive and jot down notes or significant points on which comments may be made at the designated time.

Remind Small Group Representatives of the Time. Each group representative should summarize the group's reflection in less than five minutes. Allow up to five minutes to discuss each group's presentation.

Note: If there were more than four groups, allow each group three minutes to summarize reflections and encourage small group presenters to keep their reflections within the three minutes.

LIFE APPLICATION DISCUSSION*
If time permits, the larger group can then discuss reflections on the Well Words, Well Language and Well Works sections of their workbook.
Introduction
The Life Application section consists of reflections on the Well Words, Well Language and Well Works assigned in the Student Book. Participants are asked to share which words personally framed their journey and what steps they will personally take to demonstrate the lessons learned. Discussion should also address the implications for the church as a whole.

Sharing Insights

This discussion should be open-ended and voluntary. The sharing of personal insights or recommendations for church ministry should be encouraged but not required. The group may have much to share. Be mindful of the time and dedicate only 15 minutes to this exercise.

*Answers are not provided for this section of the study because of the personal or specific nature of the reflections.

Preparation For Next Meeting

Assignment. Participants are asked to read Chapter 11, "A Woman of Value and Worth." Review the Well Lessons in preparation for the next session. Encourage them to come to the next session prepared to share their insights on the contents of the next chapter.

CLOSING PRAYER

Form a prayer circle and ask for specific prayer requests. Then ask several volunteers to pray, keeping the prayer requests in mind.

ANSWERS TO BIBLE STUDY APPLICATION

WELL LESSON #1
Learn to take advantage of and nurture opportunities.

Many times opportunities come when we least expect them. Jesus, the Christ created an opportunity for redemption when the Samaritan woman was not seeking redemption... So many opportunities... The first lesson is to learn to take advantage and make the most of every opportunity. Take a deep breath and be determined to take advantage of every opportunity and every Teachable Moment. — Vashti McKenzie

1. The following persons were called out by God and given the opportunity to serve Him. Each was shocked that God would choose them and give them an opportunity; yet each took advantage of their opportunity. Each experienced opportunities when they least expected them. Look up the following Scriptures and describe the "unexpected" opportunities that each person experienced.

Exodus 3:10-12
Moses is given the unexpected opportunity to go to Pharaoh and bring the children of Israel out of Egypt.

Isaiah 6:5-13
Isaiah is given the unexpected opportunity to be God's prophet and speak for God to the people of Israel.

Jeremiah 1:4-10
Jeremiah is given the unexpected opportunity to be God's prophet and speak for God to the people of Israel.

Mark 1:16-20
The disciples are given the unexpected opportunity to follow Jesus.

2. Describe how you know that the opportunities that were given to each of the previous persons were unexpected.

Moses:
Moses had just committed murder in Egypt and had fled in exile to Midian when God appeared to him at the burning bush. Moses could not have expected that one day he would have to return to Egypt and face the Pharaoh from whom he had fled. Neither did Moses expect to become leader of the people from whom he had fled. He asked God, "Who am I, that I should go to Pharaoh and bring the Israelites out of Egypt?" (Exodus 3:11 NIV)

Isaiah:
Upon God's call, Isaiah immediately points to his inadequacies and the inadequacies of the people - "I am a man of unclean lips, and I live among a people of unclean lips" (Isaiah 6:5 NIV). He saw these as limitations that God could not use.

Jeremiah:
Jeremiah sees his inability to speak and his youthfulness as issues that prevent him from being the prophet that God was calling him to be. Jeremiah did not expect God to be able to use him with such inadequacies.

The Disciples:
The disciples were all busy at work with their occupations, when Jesus called them to follow Him. They were given no time to prepare, just respond to the unexpected opportunity that Jesus offered.

3. In each of these unexpected moments, what assurances did the Lord give?

Exodus 3:12
God told Moses that He would go with him.

Isaiah 6:6
God sent one of the seraphs to touch and cleanse Isaiah's lips with a live coal, thereby making him holy and worthy.

Jeremiah 1:7-8
God tells Jeremiah that He will send him and instruct him on what to say. God also promises to be with Jeremiah to deliver him.

Mark 1:17
God tells these first disciples to follow him and in that command, they were given an opportunity to be with Jesus and to be directed by His divine leadership.

4. Look up the following Scriptures that point to persons who did take advantage of the opportunities given by God. Describe their missed opportunities and discuss the personal lessons you learn from each.

Genesis 6:5-8; 7:16
All of humanity, with the exception of Noah, had become sinful and God became sorry that humanity was created. Their wickedness led to God's destruction of all, except Noah, in the flood. God instructed Noah to build an ark to save himself, his family, and the selected animals, according to God's instruction. The remaining humanity missed an opportunity to be saved from the flood as God shuts the door of the ark (Genesis 7:16) and brings forth the waters of the flood. God does provide opportunities to us, but at the same time, God grieves when we fail to take of them. That grief can result in God's judgment and our destruction.

Matthew 13:54-58

The people in Jesus' own hometown of Nazareth missed an opportunity to be blessed because they did not believe that He was given favor by God to teach them. "They took offense at him," (Matthew 13:57) and because they did not believe, Jesus did not do many miracles there. When we lack faith in what the Lord can do for us, we also miss the opportunity to be blessed and to receive the many miracles that God wants to give to us.

Mark 10:17-22

The rich young ruler missed an opportunity for eternal life because of his unwillingness to sell all of his material possessions and follow Christ. His attachment to things was more important than his commitment to the Lord.

We must not let our attachment to material things get in the way of serving the Lord and cause us to miss opportunities to serve God.

Luke 22:54-62

Peter missed an opportunity to testify for Jesus when he denied three times that he knew Jesus. His missed opportunity to acknowledge the Lord led him to feel guilt and shame after realizing what he had done. The Scripture says: "he went outside and wept bitterly." We must never miss an opportunity to testify about our knowledge of Jesus.

5. There are many reasons why we miss the opportunities or teachable moments that God has planned for our lives. Dr. McKenzie calls those reasons "Learning Disabilities" because they are conditions that create difficulties for us to achieve the learning that God purposes for our lives. List some of the reasons for the missed opportunities that have occurred in your life.
Answers may include:
Fear
Low self-esteem
Past experiences
Guilt
Shame
Cultural, societal and historical definitions and limitations that you accepted

WELL LESSON #2

The Living Water Jesus provides brings you beyond the left over crumbs society has to offer.

1. Look up the Scriptures below and write how the persons moved beyond society's barriers to make the most of their opportunities.

Moses' mother (Jochebed) Exodus 2:1-10
She stepped over the society's law, hid Moses and put him in the river. She was able to nurse her child.

Jael (Judges 4:17-24)
She stepped over society's view of helpless women and helped the Israelites conquer the Canaanite army commander Sisera.

Nehemiah (Nehemiah 1:1-2:9)
Nehemiah moved beyond his role as the king's servant to seek permission to go to Jerusalem to rebuild the wall. He also received letters to protect himself and to get assistance with the project.

2. During times of crisis, disaster or grief situations, God makes possible to each a door of opportunity. We are given a chance; an opportunity; a teachable moment, in which God revealed life lessons. Look up the verses below and write what the Scriptures say about God's door of opportunity for those who served Him.

Revelation 3:8a, NIV
"I know your deeds. See, I have placed before you an open door that no one can shut."

1 Corinthians 16:9, NIV
" ... because a great door for effective work has opened to me, and there are many who oppose me."

Acts 14:27, NIV
"On arriving there, they gathered the church together and reported all that God had done through them and how he had opened the door of faith to the Gentiles."

Colossians 4:3, NIV
"And pray for us, too, that God may open a door for our message, so that we may proclaim the mystery of Christ, for which I am in chains."

WELL LESSON #3

Teachable Moments: Opportunities can be teachable moments and teachable moments can be opportunities.

Jesus skipped over her cultural prejudices, social segregation, and racial purity issues and talked to her about theological issues. Jesus thought more of her than anyone had in a long time — Vashti McKenzie

1. Use the following verses to discuss how God's door of opportunity or teachable moments were made accessible to persons who considered themselves unworthy because of cultural, societal, or physical differences.

Matthew 8:2-3
The leper thought himself unworthy and asked the Lord if He was willing to cleanse him. The Lord healed him and provided him an opportunity to live a life without the stigma of leprosy.

Luke 7:2-10
The centurion sent for Jesus to come and heal his servant, but when Jesus arrived at his home, the centurion said that because of his past, he did not feel worthy to have Jesus in his home. Jesus recognized the centurion's faith and healed his servant.

John 5:1-9
When Jesus asked the invalid if he wanted to get well, the man said he didn't have anyone to put him into the pool. Jesus used his excuse as a teachable moment and told him to get up.

Acts 3:1-8
The crippled man asked Peter and John for money. They used the opportunity to teach him the power of healing in the name of Jesus Christ.

LIFE APPLICATION
Personal Application

It is in these moments of reflection, that we must remember the Word of God and the promises and assurances that it reveals to us about taking advantage of all opportunities that the Lord gives to us.

WELL WORDS

The following Well Words are offered as encouragement you when you feel that you are not conscious of opportunities in your life. Select one Well Word per day or per week. Memorize this Well Word. It is your personal spiritual landmark to help you in your journey.

"Let the morning bring me word of your unfailing love, for I have put my trust in you. Show me the way I should go, for to you I lift up my soul" (Psalm 143:8, NIV).

"Teach me to do your will, for you are my God; may your good spirit lead me on level ground" (Psalm 143:10, NIV).

"You women who are so complacent, rise up and listen to me; you daughters who feel secure, hear what I have to say!" (Isaiah 32:9, NIV).

"The tongue has the power of life and death, and those who love it will eat its fruit." (Proverbs 18:21, NIV).

"My ears had heard of you but now my eyes sees you" (Job 42:5, NIV).

"Therefore, as we have opportunity, let us do good to all people, especially to those who belong to the family of believers" (Galatians 6:10, NIV).

"...Because a great door for effective work has opened to me, and there are many who oppose me." (1 Corinthians 16:9, NIV)

WELL SABBATICAL

Spend a portion of your regular rest and reflection period, or one entire sabbatical per week asking God to open your eyes to opportunities found along the pathway of living—the unexpected surprises missed while looking for the pot of gold at the end of the rainbow. Partner with God to seize, nurture, and make the most of all opportunities: the ones you go after, the ones you make happen, and the ones God's grace and God's will send your way. Look for ways to use one opportunity as a bridge to another.

Spend moments in your sabbatical looking toward the horizon for new opportunities, not mourning the ones you missed, messed up, or ignored, but eagerly grasping those opportunities before you.

WELL LANGUAGE

Let the following affirmations of encouragement also guide you in your journey. Write your favorite on a 3x5 or 5x7 file card in a felt-tip pen in a color you prefer.

1. I am worth it!
2. I am valuable!
3. I am becoming...
4. I have the courage to pursue God's opportunities
5. I am open to new possibilities every day
6. Problems are opportunities in disguise
7. Lord, I am ready to learn, grow and live...teach me!
8. I am awake now!

WELL WORKS

The following Well Works are provided to help you take steps to demonstrate your new commitment to live out the lessons learned in this session. Choose one or more Well Works to do during a day.

1. Take a few moments each day and look in the mirror. The look is not to adjust your halo, lipstick, hair, or check for crow's feet, wrinkles or lines. Look yourself in the eye and see the woman staring back at you. What do your eyes tell you? If you were a stranger looking into those eyes, what do your eyes tell you about this woman in the mirror? Do your eyes dance with laughter? Can you see the depth of your character? Are your eyes frightened like a deer confronted by a hunger? Are the eyes sad? Do they reflect pain or are they clouded by confusion? What do you see when you look your self in the eye?

2. Record your impressions in your journal.

3. Look through magazines and newspapers for pictures of eyes that remind you of your eyes. Cut them out and place them on your collage.

4. Now, look yourself in the eye and tell yourself the things you need to hear but no one is saying. There is no law that says you can't say them to yourself. "I'm worth it!" "I am valuable to God!" "I am loved!" "I am blessed!" "This is going to be a blessed day!" Words have power. Do not wait for someone else to speak what you need to hear. Life and death proceed from your mouth. Speak life today. Speak those things that your spirit craves.

5. Write in your journal about your teachable moments.

Church Ministry Application
- Reflect on the blessed opportunities that God has given to your church this past year.
- Have those blessed opportunities been celebrated in the worship service, preached from the pulpit, experienced by the members of the congregation?
- How faithfully are you and the members of your congregation taking advantage of all the opportunities that God has sought to bless you with?
- Pray for an attitude of gratitude that expresses joy and appreciation to the Lord for the many opportunites God has provided for your church to minister to families, communities, and the world.

A WOMAN OF VALUE AND WORTH

For sessions of 90 minutes or more, use the lesson format for PART ONE and PART TWO.

PART ONE
Opening Prayer — 5 minutes
Scripture - 15 minutes
Chapter Highlights* - 15 minutes

PART TWO
Well Lessons
Small Group - 15 minutes
Large Group - 20 minutes
Life Application* - 15 minutes
Closing Prayer - 5 minutes
•Chapter Highlights and Life Application Sections are eliminated in 60 minute Sessions.

For sessions of less than 90 minutes, the Life Application questions may be assigned as homework.

Revelation is a God-sent idea, moment, or thought. It may be an answer to a question, a solution to a question that leads to other questions and solutions, or a thought that makes clear the cloudy. It is a light in the dark. — Vashti McKenzie

Lesson Aim

At the end of this Bible Study session, participants should be able to: a) define what a revelation is; b) realize that worship is not limited to a particular space or place; c) become positioned to receive the revelation of Christ and then act on it; d) experience the benefit of true worship, i.e., have a sense of who God is and what God can do.

"God is Spirit, and his worshipers must worship in spirit and in truth" (John 4:24, NIV).

124

PART ONE

OPENING PRAYER – 5 Minutes

Begin the session with a prayer of thanksgiving for the benefits that each participant will receive who has participated in the Disciplines of the Well. Conclude the prayer with requests for God's further blessings on each participant to:

- Make meaningful worship a priority.
- Be ready to receive the revelations of Christ.
- See a loved one take a step toward personal transformation beginning with acts of personal revelation.

SCRIPTURE SEARCH – 10 Minutes

Ask the class to read in unison John 4:23-24, NIV and involve them in a discussion of the following questions, to be answered with true or false. An explanation for the reason should follow.

1. True worshipers are characterized by their style of worship. (i.e., emotional vs. quiet)

_____ True   ___X___ False

2. True worship is determined by one's sincerity and focus.

___X___ True   _____ False

3. True worshipers can be defined by where they worship.

_____ True   ___X___ False

4. Jesus said neither the mountain nor Jerusalem determines true worship. True worshipers worship in spirit and in truth.

___X___ True   _____ False

5. These are the words of Jesus. God is honored in true worship.

___X___ True   _____ False

6. Jesus said that the time had come for true worshipers to worship God.

___X___ True   _____ False

CHAPTER HIGHLIGHTS –
20 Minutes (recommended for 90-minute sessions only)

Using the content of Chapter 11 as background, give a general overview of the chapter.

Be sure to include the following areas of thought:

• Jesus treated a Samaritan woman as if she were a disciple, a religious leader, or as He would a man.

• God is spirit.

• A nameless woman, deemed unworthy by the Jews and Samaritans, was trusted with the revelation of the Messiah.

• The two revelations delivered at the well:
  Personal revelation of God, and personal revelation of self

Bible Background: The Samaritan woman needed a revelation.

The well woman's confusion was based on the traditions of the Samaritan people. Tradition said to go to Gerazim to worship. She challenged Jesus about the Jews going to Jerusalem to worship. She felt that because of this difference, the two would never be able to worship together.

Jesus took the time to explain that true worship had nothing to do with the place. Neither of the two places (Gerazim or Jerusalem) were the basis for worship. Instead, He explained, "worship must be done in spirit and in truth."

PART TWO

BIBLE STUDY APPLICATION
Introduction

The Bible Study Application section contains four Well Lessons, which teach the importance of spending time with Jesus in worship for discovery of God and one's self. The discussion of the Well Lessons should confirm the fact of spirit and truth being the essence of true worship. Allow students time to explore the Well Lessons, sharing concepts and thoughts.

Procedure

Select Small Group Leaders. Ask for volunteers or select four small group leaders and assign a number to each leader. Ask the small group leaders to write their numbers on large sheets of white paper so that they can be seen from a distance. (This can also be done beforehand to save time).

Divide into Small Groups. Inform the participants that they will be separated into four groups. Each group will study a different Well Lesson and then present their reflections to the larger group at the end of the study period. The Well Lessons should be assigned as follows:

Group 1: Spending time with Jesus is an experience in revelation that increases our sense of who God is and what God can do.

Group 2: Your test may become your testimony.

Group 3: You are a person of value and worth.

Group 4: Everyone does not have the same theophany, but you can still go to the well.

Allow participants to count off by fours. Then ask them to follow the small group leader who is holding their assigned number. Identify the location of each group. (These locations can also be pre-printed on a sheet of paper, photocopied, and distributed to save time.) Participants should then gather into smaller groups in the designated meeting areas.

Note: If the Bible study is large, divide into more groups and reassign alternately the same four Well Lessons to each of the additional groups. In this case, possibly more than one group will be reflecting on each of the Well Lessons. If the Bible Study is small, remain in one group to discuss all four Well Lessons.

Small Group Study
Small Group Leaders
Each group will have one Well Lesson to explore. For each Well Lesson, there will be related Scripture references to stimulate discussion.

Sharing Insights
After 15 minutes, designate someone to summarize the small group discussion within the large group presentation that follows. The designated person will have five minutes to present.

Large Group Presentations
Reconvene the Group. Call the small groups together.

Explain the Procedure. A representative from each of the small groups will share that group's reflections on the Well Lesson assigned. The large group will have an opportunity to comment on reflections after all presentations have been made. Remind participants of the large group to be attentive and jot down notes or significant points on which comments may be made at the designated time.

Remind Small Group Representatives of the Time. Each group representative should summarize the group's reflection in less than five minutes. Allow up to five minutes to discuss each group's presentation.

Note: If there were more than four groups, allow each group three minutes to summarize reflections and encourage small group presenters to keep their reflections within the three minutes.

LIFE APPLICATION DISCUSSION*

If time permits, the larger group can then discuss reflections on the Well Words, Well Language and Well Works sections of their workbook.

Introduction

The Life Application section consists of reflections on the Well Words, Well Language and Well Works assigned in the Student Book. Participants are asked to share which words personally framed their journey and what steps they will personally take to demonstrate the lessons learned. Discussion should also address the implications for the church as a whole.

Sharing Insights

This discussion should be open-ended and voluntary. The sharing of personal insights or recommendations for church ministry should be encouraged but not required. The group may have much to share. Be mindful of the time and dedicate only 10 minutes to this exercise.

*Answers are not provided for this section of the study because of the personal or specific nature of the reflections.

Preparation For Next Meeting

Assignment. Participants are asked to read Chapter 12, "A Woman With a Purpose." Review the Well Lessons in preparation for the next session. Encourage them to come to the next session prepared to share their insights on the content of the next chapter.

The leader may also want to assign small groups or specific Well Lessons to facilitate next week's meeting time.

CLOSING PRAYER

Invite all to pray individually for the passion to worship God in spirit and in truth — thereby getting to know God more personally. Leader may choose to close with a prayer of thanksgiving for what God is doing for each participant through the Disciplines of the Well.

ANSWERS TO BIBLE STUDY APPLICATION

WELL LESSON #1

Spending time with Jesus is an experience in revelation that increases our sense of who God is and what God can do.

"God is Spirit, and his worshipers must worship in spirit and in truth' (John 4:24, NIV).

1. The following Scripture references talk about people who received various revelations about / from God. Describe the person's reaction in each case.

Psalm 138:2
David indicated that during his praise, God's name and his word were exalted above everything else.

Deuteronomy 29:29
The writer received God's purpose for revealing the word to us. He says it is for us and our children to obey.

Exodus 34:34
The children of Israel observed a change in Moses' face (countenance) after he was in the presence of God. The Scripture says that it was "aglow."

2. Look up the following passages of Scripture to review certain attributes of God, which when revealed, help us to worship more fully.

Psalm 90:2
ETERNAL — The Psalmist writes that before there were mountains, the earth, or the world, God was/is.

Psalm 139:7-12
OMNIPRESENT — The Psalmist declares that God is everywhere and there is no place that he can go to escape God's presence.

1 Peter 1:16
HOLINESS — God is holy. He is perfect — without blemish. God's perfect nature precludes the possibility of inconsistency in truth.

Psalm 19:9
JUSTICE — God's administration of the law is fair and right. God rewards and penalizes people according to their choices.

Psalm 23:6
GOODNESS — God's goodness and mercy is promised forever.

Hebrews 11:11
FAITHFULNESS — God can be depended on to keep promises made to believers.

3. Locate relevant passages of Scripture to confirm what you know about other attributes of God.

Omnipotent	**Matthew 19:26**
Omniscient	**Isaiah 42:8, 9**
Immutability	**James 1:17**
Spirituality	**John 4:24**

WELL LESSON #2
Your test may become your testimony.

1. Read the following accounts of tests. How would the person say the test became their testimony.

John 9:1-7
The man's test was that he was born blind. When Jesus healed him, his test became his testimony.

John 8:1-11
The woman's test was getting caught in her sin and being paraded into court by Pharisees. Her test became a testimony when she met Jesus, who did not condemn her but told her to sin no more.

Genesis 22:1-14

Abraham's test was being obedient to God by offering his son as a sacrifice. His test became a testimony when God provided a ram in the bush.

WELL LESSON #3
You are a person of value and worth.

Jesus trusted the revelation to a woman deemed unworthy by both the Jews and Samaritans. He trusted a vital spiritual revelation to a woman who could not get her relationship issues right. — Vashti McKenzie

Jesus showed by His actions the worth of a woman who had little value to anyone else. Even today, many things are used to determine the value of a person. Often opportunities are scarcer for minorities than for other groups.

1. Review the following Scripture passages for a study on how God feels about the worth of people.

Psalm 8:5, 6
Man/woman is made a little lower than angels.
Man/woman is crowned with glory and honor
Man/woman has been given dominion over the earth.
God has put everything under their feet.

Genesis 1:26, 27
Man/woman is made in the Divine image

2. Match the following verses with persons who thought little of themselves for various reasons. What were their outcomes?

a. Luke 15:19   **Prodigal Son; His father received him**
b. Matthew 15:27   **Canaanite woman whose daughter needed healing; her daughter was healed**
c. Luke 23:42   **Thief on the cross; Jesus thought enough of him to save him**

WELL LESSON #4

Everyone does not have the same theophany, but you can still go to the well.

How do you get to the well? The journey begins in prayer. It is expanded in worship and explored in study. — *Vashti McKenzie*

1. Examine how you and each of your group members has journeyed to the well. How did the journey begin? What are some of the results? *Answers will vary.*

LIFE APPLICATION

Personal Application

Plan to visit a church of another ethnic group or denomination.

Write your thoughts upon entering the church and your thoughts upon leaving.

During your moments of reflection, keep in mind what Jesus said about the components of true worship of God: Spirit and truth.

WELL WORDS

The following Well Words will help you in times of worship.

"Worship the Lord in the splendor of his holiness, tremble before him, all the earth" (Psalm 99:5, NIV).

"Come let us bow down in worship, let us kneel before the Lord our Maker" (Psalm 95:6, NIV).

"...Worship the Lord your God, and serve him only" (Matthew 4:10b, NIV).

"And they stayed at the temple continually praising God" (Luke 24:53, NIV).

"Worship the Lord with gladness; come before him with joyful songs" (Psalm 100:2, NIV).

"Enter his gates with thanksgiving and his courts with praise; give thanks to him and praise his name" (Psalm 100:4, NIV).

"I will declare your name to my brothers and sisters, in the presence of the congregation I will sing your praises" (Hebrews 2:12, NIV).

WELL SABBATICAL

Spend your sabbatical seasons in worship. First, set aside a daily time to spend in private worship. The presence of God is ushered in on the shoulders of praise, as God inhabits the praises of His people (Psalm). Praise is acclamation and adoration. It is verbally giving honor to God. If you are not quite sure how to begin, read praise passages from the Book of Psalms such as: "I will extol the Lord at all times; his praise will always be on my lips. My soul will boast in the Lord; let the afflicted hear and rejoice. Glorify the Lord with me; let us exalt his name together (Psalm 34:1-3, NIV). "Let me live so I may praise you..." (Psalm 119:175) or the praise crescendos of Psalm 150.

After praising God, thank God for who He is, what He has done, and what He is doing. Use Psalm 103 to begin your time of thanksgiving. "Praise the Lord, O my soul; all my inmost being, praise his holy name. Praise the Lord, O my soul, and forget not all his benefits—who forgives all your sins and heals all your diseases, who redeems your life from the pit and crowns you with love and compassion, who satisfies your desires with good things so that your youth is renewed like the eagle's (Psalm 103:1-5, NIV).

Do not ask God to do anything for you. Save your prayer requests and concerns. Spend the balance of your sabbatical in private worship, reaching for the heart of God in praise and thanksgiving, not petitioning.

WELL LANGUAGE

1. I am a person of value. I am a person of worth.
2. I will praise the Lord at all times.
3. With my whole heart will I praise the Lord!
4. Magnify the Lord with me and together we give God praise!
5. Give God the praise!
6. Worship is my strength.
7. God is a spirit and I worship Him in spirit and in truth.
8. Worship is my reach to God; blessing is the return.
9. God looks beyond my faults to my needs.
10. Lord, I am available to you!

11. I love the Lord!
12. I can worship! Come magnify the Lord with me.
13. I will praise the Lord with my whole heart!

WELL WORKS

1. Make the decision to attend a corporate worship setting of your choice. If you usually attend Sabbath worship, attend a mid-week service during the day or evening. Spending time with Jesus in worship is an experience in revelation.
2. In your journal, write a love letter to the Lord. Share why you love the Lord, including a list of the many ways you can demonstrate your love for Him. Be open and honest, and express yourself fully.
3. Read 1 Peter 2 and list what the Bible says about you.
4. Look at Vessels of Honor in the concordance of your Study Bible or Bible Dictionary.
5. Create your own valentine for Jesus and add it to your collage.

Church Ministry Application

Encourage a fellowship service with your church and another church of a different denomination.

Invite the youth of other churches in the area to combine with your church in a community project. (Get permission from your church and participating churches first).

A WOMAN WITH A PURPOSE

For sessions of 90 minutes or more, use the lesson format for PART ONE and PART TWO.

When you don't know your purpose, then you serve others and their idea for life, not God's intended purpose for you." — Vashti McKenzie

PART ONE

Opening Prayer - 5 minutes

Scripture Search - 15 minutes

Chapter Highlights* - 15 minutes

PART TWO

Well Lessons

Small Group - 15 minutes

Large Group - 20 minutes

Life Application* - 15 minutes

Closing Prayer - 5 minutes

*Chapter Highlights and Life Application Sections are eliminated in 60 minute Sessions

For sessions of less than 90 minutes, the Life Application questions may be assigned as homework.

Lesson Aim

At the end of this Bible study session, the participants should: a) be able to distinguish between one's assumed purpose (other's expectations) and one's "Created Purpose"; b) begin a personal search through prayer, fasting and the Word to identify their "Created Purpose"; c) Reflect on a personal defining moment.

"Then, leaving her water jar, the woman went back to the town and said to the people, 'Come, see a man who told me everything I ever did'" (John 4:28-29, NIV).

OPENING PRAYER – 5 Minutes

Open the session with a prayer of thanksgiving for each member of the class and the "Journey" which all have shared these past weeks. Ask four

135

people to share in the prayer. Pray that each class member will:
- Seek to know their "Created Purpose."
- Use life's experiences to grow
- Acknowledge Christ as the transforming power of their lives
- Thank God for meeting them on their "journey"
  (Each prayer person will pray for one of the above needs.)

SCRIPTURE SEARCH –15 minutes

Ask someone to read John 4:28-30 and ask the following questions:

1. Where did the woman go when she left the well?
She went back into the city.

2. What did she do with her water jar?
She left it.

3. What did she do when she got into the town?
She invited the people to come to meet Jesus.

4. What was the response of the people?
They followed her out of the town to meet Jesus.

Discuss what happened to make her believe that Jesus must be the Christ. Include the following points:

1. Jesus knew her past without having met her before

2. Jesus told her that He was the Messiah.

3. Jesus took the time to talk to her — even though they were of different races — He was a Jew and she was a Samaritan.

Entertain discussion on why the Samaritan woman was likely to tell others about Jesus.

1. She had experienced her defining moment and wanted to share what had happened to her.

2. She felt no restraints, having been freed from racial, religious and gender barriers.

3. Telling others about Jesus was her created purpose.

CHAPTER HIGHLIGHTS

Using the content of Chapter 12 as background, give a general overview of the chapter. Be sure to include the following topics:

1. The revelation of the Son of God became a life-changing experience for the Samaritan woman.
2. Defining moments have the power to change our lives.
3. The woman's sermon, "Come and see a man" affected a whole town.
4. There are many women inside of us.
5. An appropriate evaluation of one's self occurs when seen through the eyes of Jesus.

PART TWO

BIBLE STUDY APPLICATION

Introduction

The Bible Study Application section contains three Well Lessons that provide an opportunity to examine what the Bible says about searching for and finding our "Created Purpose." Allow as much time as possible to encourage free participation and exchange of ideas and insights.

Procedure

Select Small Group Leaders. Ask for volunteers or select three small group leaders and assign each leader a number from 1-3. Ask the small group leaders to write their number on large sheets of paper so that they can be seen from a distance. (This can also be done beforehand to save time).

Divide into small groups. Inform the participants that they will be separated into small groups. Each group will reflect on a different Well Lesson and then present their reflections to the larger group at the end of the study period. The Well Lessons should be assigned as follows:

Group 1: Pay attention to defining moments. (Well Lesson #1)

Group 2: Purpose is the permanent thread that weaves through every aspect of existence. (Well Lesson #2)

Group 3: The Journey Continues (Well lesson #3)

Allow participants to count off by threes. Then ask them to follow the small group leader who is holding their assigned number. Identify the location of each group. (These locations can also be pre-printed on a sheet of paper, photocopied, and distributed to save time). Participants should then gather into smaller groups in the designated meeting areas.

Note: If the Bible Study is large, divide into more groups and reassign alternately the same three Well Lessons to each of the additional groups. In this case, possibly more than one group will be reflecting on each of the Well Lessons. If the Bible Study is small, divide into two groups and permit each group to discuss as many of the reflections as each group desires. You may also want to include Well Lesson 3 as part of the homework assignment.

Small Group Study
Small Group Leaders
Each group will have one Well Lesson to explore. For each Well Lesson, there are questions and/or related Scripture references to stimulate discussion.

Sharing Insights
After 15 minutes, designate someone to summarize the small group discussion within the large group presentation that follows. The designated person will have five minutes to present.

Large Group Presentations
Reconvene the Group. Call the groups together.

Explain the Procedure. A representative from each of the small groups will share that group's reflections on the Well Lesson assigned. The large group will be given an opportunity to comment on reflections after all presentations have been made. Remind participants of the large group to be attentive and jot down notes or significant points on which comments may be made at the designated time.

Remind Small Group Representatives of the Time. Each group representative should summarize the group's reflection in less than five minutes. Allow up to five minutes to discuss each group's presentation.

Note: If there are more than four groups, allow each group three minutes to summarize reflections and encourage small group presenters to keep their reflections within the three minutes.

LIFE APPLICATION DISCUSSION

If time permits, the larger group can then discuss reflections on the Well Words, Well Language and Well Works section of their workbook.

Introduction

The Life Application section consists on reflections on the Well Words, Well Language and Well Works assigned in the Student Book. Participants are asked to share which words personally framed their journey and what steps they will personally take to demonstrate the lessons learned. Discussion should also address the implications for the church as a whole.

Sharing Insights

This discussion should be open-ended and voluntary. The sharing of personal insights or recommendations for church ministry should be encouraged but not required. The group may have much to share. Be mindful of the time and dedicate only 15 minutes to this exercise. *Answers are not provided for this section of the study because of the personal or specific nature of the reflections.

CLOSING PRAYER

Form a prayer circle and ask each member of the class for a "sentence prayer." The prayer can then be closed with thanksgiving for all who have participated in the "Journey" experience and for what this will mean in their lives and the lives of others.

ANSWERS TO BIBLE STUDY APPLICATION

WELL LESSON #1
Pay attention to defining moments.

By being aware, you can make the most of your intended purpose
— Vashti McKenzie

"Then, leaving her water jar, the woman went back to the town and said to the people, 'Come, see a man who told me everything I ever did'" (John 4:28-29, NIV).

"Amazing Grace! How sweet the sound, that saved a wretch like me! I once was lost, but now am found, was blind but now I see."

John Newton, a former slave trader is said to have written these words. They were the result of an out-to-sea experience in a life-threatening storm. As a slave trader, he transported people from West Africa to be sold as slaves in slave markets around the world. It is unimaginable that such a person would give any thought to repentance and salvation. But he did! A book, "The Imitation of Christ" by Thomas Kempis and fear of the storm was the cause of Newton's transformation. Newton died at age 82. He, like so many others, was grateful for the grace of God and continued to pen his feelings in other songs.

1. The brief biographies below contain facts about Bible personalities who experienced transformation during defining moments. After reading their stories, write their names on the lines below.

1. Loved Jesus.
2. Observed the crucifixion along with Mary, the mother of Jesus. (Luke 23:49)
3. Was delivered from demons by Jesus. (Luke 8:2)
4. The first to witness the resurrected Lord. (John 20:1-18)
(Mary Magdalene)

Luke 19:1-10
He had a passion to meet Jesus.
Jesus invited himself to this man's house.

He offered to give one-half of his belongings to the poor and to return fourfold all that he had wrongfully taken from other people.
Received salvation on the day that he met Jesus.
 (Zacchaeus)

Acts 8:26-38
Sought to understand the Prophet Isaiah's writings (53:7, 8) concerning Jesus.

Came from Ethiopia
Asked Philip to help him understand the Scriptures
After instruction, believed that Jesus Christ is the Son of God
(Ethiopian Eunuch)

Acts 13:7-12
Wanted to hear the word of the Lord
Proconsul or Roman deputy of Cyprus
Believed after seeing Elymas or Barjesus struck with blindness

Sent for Barnabas and Saul/Paul to instruct him in the word of the Lord

Was amazed at the teachings regarding the Lord
(Sergius Paulus)

Acts 16:14-15
Lived in Thyatira
Worshipped God
Invited Paul to her home
She and her household were baptized by Paul after hearing the message of Jesus
(Lydia)

2. There is a common thread in all of the above stories. Write what you think it might be.
They were open to transformation / change and paid attention to their defining moments.

3. What is there in each of the stories that would indicate these people had experienced personal transformation in their beliefs and behaviors?
Each person did something positive following the change that had taken place.

WELL LESSON #2
Purpose is the permanent thread that weaves through every aspect of existence.

Purpose...is the answer to questions of "Why was I born?" and "Why am I here?" — Vashti McKenzie

Referring to the book *Journey to the Well*, discuss the following:

1. Jesus' statement to the disciples in answer to their concern that He had not eaten. "My food is to do the will of him who sent me and to complete his work." In what way would this statement be reflective of Jesus' purpose?
His purpose was to do the will of God which was to reach the lost. He indicated this in the parable of the fields that were waiting to be harvested.

2. The Samaritan woman's appeal to the folks in Samaria, "Come see a man......" was very effective in that they responded to the appeal.
How does this relate to Dr. McKenzie's concept of living a decisive life?
She says that living a decisive life is to find meaning beyond the limitations of self. This woman, after having received Jesus herself, went out to bring others.

3. In your own words, write what you think Dr. McKenzie means by "Created Purpose?"
Answers will vary.

WELL LESSON #3
The Journey Continues.

As the cycles of life ebb and flow, as our circumstances change and new well moments present themselves, the journey continues. — Vashti McKenzie

Choose one of the Bible personalities studied throughout this course. Use Scripture references to chart their journey to the well. How were they transformed? What change did they make after their defining moment? How does their journey relate to yours?

LIFE APPLICATION
Personal Application
It is in these moments of reflection, that we must remember the Word of God and the power of a transformed life in living up to our "Created Purpose."

WELL WORDS

The following Well Words are offered as encouragement when you have difficulty living up to your Created Purpose.

"And we know that in all things God works for the good of those who love him, who have been called according to his purpose" (Romans 8:28, NIV).

"...I have raised you up for this very purpose, that I might show you my power and that my name might be proclaimed in all the earth." (Exodus 9:16, NIV)

"Many are the plans in a man's heart, but it is the Lord's purpose that prevails." (Proverbs 19:21, NIV)

"so is my word that goes from my mouth: it will not return to me empty, but will accomplish what I desire and achieve the purpose for which I sent it." (Isaiah 55:11, NIV)

"Now it is God who has made us for this very purpose and has given us the Spirit as a deposit, guaranteeing what is to come..." (2 Corinthians 5:5, NIV)

"It is fine to be zealous, provided the purpose is good, and to be so always and not just when I am with you." (Galatians 4:18, NIV)

"In him we were also chosen, having been predestined according to the plan of him who works out everything in conformity with the purpose of his will." (Ephesians 1:11, NIV)

"...then make my joy complete by being like-minded, having the same love, being one in spirit and purpose." (Philippians 2:2, NIV)

"...who has saved us and called us to a holy life-not because of anything we have done but because of his own purpose and grace. This grace was given us in Christ Jesus before the beginning of time." (2 Timothy 1:9, NIV)

WELL SABBATICAL

Remember that the degree to which you pursue your rest period is the degree of the reward you receive for the time spent with the Lord. All too often we allow whims, fancies, and desires to lead us in doing, before we know the why of our doing. Use the Scriptures from Well Words as you seek the Lord's guidance to Created Purpose identification. God is not playing a game, keeping purpose a mysterious secret.

WELL LANGUAGE
1. Think decisively; live on purpose
2. My purpose is why God created me.
3. Get involved in a cause greater than yourself.
4. It is not who you are but who you are willing to become.
5. Purpose and persistence, don't leave home without it!
6. Competence needs courage and confidence to perform
7. There is a reason to my being! Live on purpose.

WELL WORKS
Take the next few days to identify the permanent thread that is woven through every person on the inside of you. Kevin W. McCarthy describes an excellent method of uncovering purpose in the book "The On-Purpose Person." In it he suggests making a want list in eight different categories. The topics include Spiritual, Financial/Material, Family, Vocation/Career, Social/Community, Mental/Intellectual, Physical/Health/Recreational, and Other.

Write your list of wants as fully as possible, consolidating categories if necessary. In each category compare the wants with each other to determine which is more important, until you get down to one core want in each category. The author then suggests that you compare the core want in each category until you identify one that is more important than the other eight. The final core is your main purpose. The exercise is not final. It can be repeated.

Your last assignment is to write your own poem or story of transformation. It is your declaration of freedom in Jesus Christ. It is your Magna Carta of self-definition and spiritual actualization. It is your dialogue.

Church Ministry Application
Consider a study of your church's mission statement (the church's purpose) by each member.

Suggest that a copy be made available to everyone.

Suggest that it be run in the church bulletin or newsletter for a period of time. This study might aid the church in being on target in planning the church programs.